CREATIVE
DO IT YOURSELF

Garden
Building Projects

WARD LOCK

© Ward Lock Limited, 1994
A Cassell Imprint
Villiers House, 41-47 Strand, London WC2N 5JE

Based on *Successful DIY*
© Eaglemoss Publications Limited, 1994

ISBN 0 7063 7276 X

Printed in Spain by Cayfosa Industria Grafica

10 9 8 7 6 5 4 3 2 1

CONTENTS

INTRODUCTION

FOR THOSE people lucky enough to have a garden, a whole new area of do-it-yourself activity beckons. Such outdoor DIY jobs are generally more forgiving than indoor ones since making a bit of a mess and achieving less-than-perfect results don't matter quite so much. So although laying bricks or concrete may seem daunting, there's no reason to feel discouraged so long as you start off with a relatively modest job. This book opens with a guide to the tools and equipment you are likely to need for outdoor building and carpentry work. This includes a number of simple tools which you can make yourself, such as a builder's square to keep corners at perfect right-angles and a simple brick gauge to keep mortar courses to an even thickness. It then digresses for a moment, with information on how to install an outside tap – essential if you are going to be mixing up mortar and concrete, and useful for watering the garden too.

The next section concentrates on basic techniques: how to set out and level a site for anything from a patio to a conservatory, how to mix mortar and concrete and how to lay a simple concrete slab. It includes useful mixing charts that enable you to gauge accurately the quantities of materials you will need for a range of bricklaying and concreting projects, so you will neither run out of materials nor waste money by ordering more than necessary.

The book then deals with paving, explaining how to use materials as diverse as concrete, paving slabs and interlocking block pavers to lay paths, patios and driveways. To help you create the perfect patio, there are special sections on patio design and on choosing and fitting a patio awning.

Boundaries and screen walls are covered next, with separate sections on using screen walling blocks – the easiest type of masonry for the builder to work with – and on repairing and erecting timber fencing. Fence maintenance covers everything from replacing rotten posts or boards to repairing broken arris rails and curing problems with wooden gates. This is followed by a guide to choosing and estimating new fencing materials, planning fence runs and preparing the site, and instructions for erecting panel and boarded fences and hanging a gate.

Finally, the book tackles two larger-scale projects. The first, erecting a prefabricated garden shed, is a relatively simple job involving little more than bolting the panels together and felting the roof. The second, adding a conservatory, is a major home improvement and the book provides a guide to choosing the right style for your home, looks at the rules and regulations involved and gives useful guidance on safety glazing, lighting, heating and ventilation, shade, and choosing conservatory flooring and furniture.

CHOOSING AND USING BUILDING TOOLS

Even as a keen do-it-yourselfer, there's little point in collecting a comprehensive set of building tools. Many of them are costly, bulky or highly specialized, and since you're unlikely to be doing building work on a daily basis it makes better sense to hire or borrow what you need as the occasion demands.

Some building tools *are* worth buying though, mainly because they have a host of other uses – for example a bolster, club hammer and a long spirit level. There are also quite a few pieces of equipment which you can make yourself, using odd pieces of scrap timber.

Value for money?

With building tools that you buy yourself, the old rule 'get the best you can afford' doesn't necessarily apply. Items such as trowels, chisels and levels vary widely in price, and the top-quality professional versions tend to be very expensive indeed. To a builder who uses such tools every day, it's worth paying the extra; for occasional DIY use it most definitely isn't.

Trade tip

Caring for tools

❝ Most building tools are designed to take a fair amount of battering about, but they quickly become ruined if left encrusted with mortar or allowed to go rusty.

After any mortar or concreting job, make a point of hosing down every piece of equipment using an old washing up brush to dislodge caked-on mud or cement.

Leave metal tools to dry, then wipe down the blades with a cloth dipped in cooking oil or light machine oil. ❞

The basic building tool kit shown here shouldn't prove costly to buy – and most items have many uses in general DIY as well as in working with concrete or mortar.

MEASURING AND LEVELLING TOOLS

Builder's spirit levels are longer and more robust than woodworker's levels – important where you need to level accurately over relatively long distances. Nowadays, they are usually made of plastic or coated aluminium.

Two common sizes are 600mm (2′) and 900mm (3′). If you can afford it, a longer one is handy on all sorts of jobs – but you still need a shorter level for carpentry and joinery.

An angle-finder on a spirit level, built in or attached, enables it to be used for setting gradients too. Alternatively, tape a spacer of the correct thickness to one end (see below).

A straightedge is the one tool which everybody improvises. A straight batten is perfectly adequate, but many builders shun timber in favour of a length of 50mm (2″) I-section aluminium strip about 2m (6′) long. Ask your builder's merchant what's available.

Mason's steel pins and twine are used for setting out excavations and checking that courses of brickwork are running level. You can do without the pins (use wooden pegs or skewers) but not the twine; ordinary household string stretches when used in this way.

Builder's water levels are used for levelling over long distances – such as when putting up a fence. You can easily make your own by adapting an ordinary garden hose (see page 10).

Builder's squares are generally pressed out of sheet metal, but you can make your own from thin strips of batten.

angle attachment

spirit level

straightedge

mason's steel pins and twine

water level

builder's square

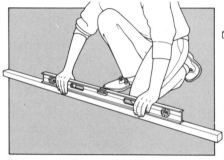

Extend the reach of a spirit level with a straightedge.

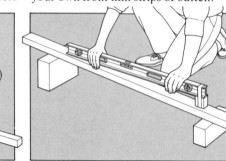

To gauge gradients, tape a block under a spirit level.

MIXING AND CARRYING EQUIPMENT

builder's bucket

spotboard

hawk

shovel

builder's barrow

cement mixer

Builder's buckets, made of robust black PVC and holding 14 litres (3 gallons), are invaluable for any sort of mortar or concrete mixing job. They are cheap to buy, so it's worth getting three; keep one exclusively for water.

Scoop-shaped buckets allow dry ingredients to be scooped up and measured at the same time without the need for shovelling.

A spotboard is essential for mixing mortar and concrete, and you can easily make your own (see page 10). However, a plastic 'no-mess' spotboard is a good buy if you're mixing indoors.

Hawks for carrying mortar and plaster are available in traditional metal and easy-to-clean plastic. They are easy to make yourself (see page 10).

Shovels are essential for concreting – and much better than the garden spade. Buy two – one for measuring ingredients and one for mixing.

Wheelbarrows can be the ordinary garden type, but if you are intending to carry bricks, buy or hire a builder's barrow – they have wider tyres to stop them sinking into soft ground.

A cement mixer takes much of the effort out of bricklaying. An electric one with a capacity of about 125 litres will operate from a 13A socket. Hire rather than buy, except for a major project – then it might be cheaper to buy, and resell afterwards.

TROWELS AND SPREADERS

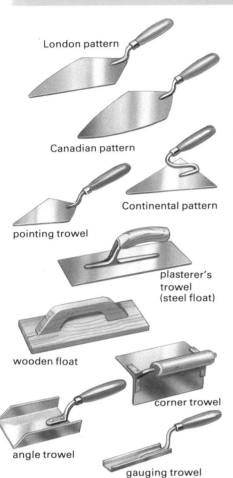

London pattern

Canadian pattern

Continental pattern

pointing trowel

plasterer's trowel (steel float)

wooden float

corner trowel

angle trowel

gauging trowel

Bricklayer's trowels come in a wide variety of shapes and sizes, based on traditional designs.

London pattern trowels have a diamond shaped blade with one straight edge (for scraping off mortar) and one curved edge for cutting bricks. They are sold 'handed', a right-handed trowel having the curved edge on the right as you look down the handle.

Canadian pattern trowels look similar, but both edges are straight.

Continental pattern trowels have triangular blades with a rounded tip.

For the do-it-yourselfer there is little to choose between the different patterns. A blade length of 225–250mm (9–10″) is a good general-purpose size.

Pointing trowels look like Canadian pattern bricklayer's trowels but are much smaller and lighter. The blade has two straight edges, and may have a pointed or rounded tip according to the type of pointing it's being used for. Blade length varies from around 100mm to 175mm (4–7″); 150mm (6″) is a good size, allowing the trowel to be used for small mortaring jobs too.

Plasterer's trowels (steel floats) have a flat steel blade – generally around 250×125mm (10×5″) – with a riveted or welded-on handle of wood or plastic. They are among the most versatile of all building tools, with countless uses wherever mortar and concrete have to be applied to a vertical surface or trowelled smooth.

The main consideration when choosing a plasterer's trowel is weight, which varies considerably. Professionals often use a heavy trowel for applying and a lighter one for smoothing. As a do-it-yourselfer, it's best to compare weights in the shop and then opt for a medium-weight trowel – when smoothing, the extra weight helps keep the blade steady and stop the edges digging in.

Specialist plastering trowels include: **Corner trowels**, with a right-angled blade for finishing external corners. **Angle**, **edging** and **gauging trowels**, which come in a range of shapes for finishing internal corners and other awkward spots. An angle trowel (or *plasterer's twitcher*) has scoop sides for catching trimmed-off mortar.

Wooden floats, used to give a slightly roughened surface finish to concrete and to apply undercoat plaster.

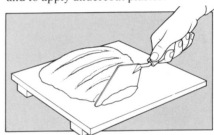

Get used to how a trowel behaves by chopping and turning some mortar before starting the job.

TOOLS FOR CUTTING

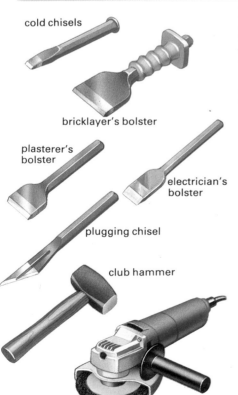

cold chisels

bricklayer's bolster

plasterer's bolster

electrician's bolster

plugging chisel

club hammer

angle grinder

Hardened steel chisels – technically all known as *cold chisels* – are the builder's main cutting tools.

Cold chisels are generally taken to be the narrow, straight-bladed type with a blade width of between 10mm (⅜″) and 38mm (1½″). They are mainly used for clearing out old pointing, and hacking away mortar in awkward corners; 25mm (1″) is a good general purpose size but buy a narrower one if repointing.

Bolsters – wide-bladed cold chisels – are virtually indispensable for DIY work; their uses include hacking off plaster, cutting bricks, blocks and pavers, levering up floorboards and stripping old decorations.

A *bricklayer's bolster* has the widest blade – commonly 75–100mm (3–4″) – and is relatively blunt; it smashes rather than cuts. A *plasterer's bolster* is sharper, with a blade width of around 50–63mm (2–2½″), and is more useful for general DIY. Sharpest of all is the *electrician's bolster*, with a blade width of 25–38mm (1–1½″); use one of these to cut neat channels in plaster, or to prise up soft floor tiles.

Plugging chisels are specialist cold chisels with angled, fluted blades for clearing out mortar joints.

A club hammer (lump hammer) is the standard tool for driving cold chisels. There are various weights, heavier hammers being more effective but also more tiring to use. For general DIY, the 3lb (1.3kg) size is best.

Angle grinders are power tools with abrasive wheels that make light work of cutting virtually any building material (and the limbs of the user!). There are two common sizes, 4½″ (112mm) and 9″ (225mm) – the diameter of the cutting wheel. The smaller size will cope with most DIY jobs, but it's usually better to hire.

Angle grinders must be used with extreme caution – particularly at the start of a cut – as they are difficult to control. Wear full protective gear, including stout shoes and gloves.

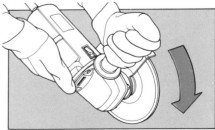

Hold an angle grinder securely and start it before touching it to the work or it may snatch.

DEMOLITION TOOLS

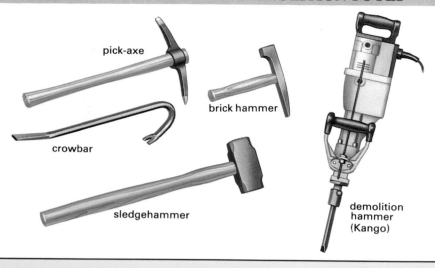

pick-axe

brick hammer

crowbar

sledgehammer

demolition
hammer
(Kango)

Pick-axes are among the most tried and tested of all building tools, but it's unlikely to be worth buying one new – hire or borrow instead.

Brick hammers are specialist tools, and again aren't worth buying new.

A crowbar is an inexpensive and versatile tool for levering and pulling.

Sledgehammers are seldom worth buying new, but it's useful to have one around if you can acquire it cheaply.

Demolition hammers – variously known as heavy duty hammer drills, percussion drills, or 'Kangos' (after the famous brand name) – are the automatic choice for breaking up large lumps of masonry or concrete. Even builders tend to prefer hiring to buying.

TOOLS TO MAKE YOURSELF

Make a builder's square from three lengths of 50×12mm (2×½") planed softwood, pinned together so that the outer edges are in the proportions shown (thus creating an exact right angle). Afterwards, saw off the overlapping corners.

For a more substantial tool use thicker timber. Pin the lengths together, mark where they cross, then pull the square apart and cut half-lap joints. Pin and glue.

Make a water level from a length of ordinary garden hose. Buy two 300mm (12") lengths of clear plastic tube thin enough to wedge inside the hose, plus a pair of corks to bung the ends.

Assemble the water level as shown. Fix tape markers halfway down the clear tubes, then fill with water up to the level of the marks and fit the bungs. Remove them to use the tool.

Make a hawk from a piece of 12mm (½") plywood about 300mm (12") square. Glue and screw a piece of squarely sawn broom handle in the middle to act as a handle. Use epoxy resin, and countersink then fill over the screw head.

For a more robust tool, nail a piece of 75×25mm (3×1") softwood to the underside of the board, then drill a suitably sized housing for the broom handle and glue in place.

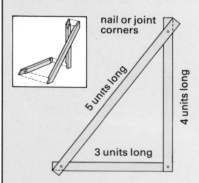

nail or joint corners

5 units long

4 units long

3 units long

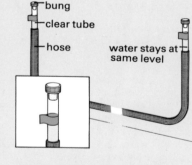

bung

clear tube

hose

water stays at same level

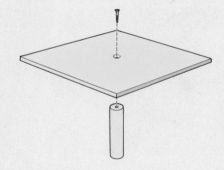

Make a spotboard for mixing mortar and concrete from a piece of 19mm blockboard or plywood about 600mm (2') square. Nail two lengths of 100×50mm (4×2") softwood underneath to act as bearers, or rest the board on bricks.

Make a brick gauge as a guide to accurate bricklaying from a straight batten. Set it against an existing brick wall and mark the thicknesses of the bricks and the mortar joints. Use this to check that bricks are being laid evenly.

Make a rammer (punner) from a length of stout fence post drilled across and fitted with a handle made from a short length of broomstick. Use it by jumping it up and down to compact earth and hardcore.

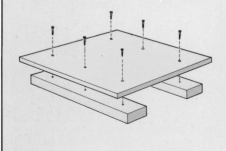

brick thickness

joint thickness

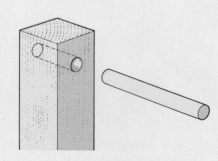

FITTING AN OUTSIDE TAP

The convenience of having a permanent water supply outdoors will more than repay the small outlay in time and materials. At its simplest, the job merely involves running a branch supply pipe through an outside wall to a tap mounted on the other side. But this section also covers running a supply to a nearby garage or outhouse, and describes how to fit a standpipe for situations where a conventional outside tap would be unsuitable.

What the Byelaws say

There are strict Water Byelaws concerning outside taps, most of which are designed to protect the mains supply from contamination or wastage, and the outside pipework from frost damage. It is illegal to disregard them.

From a do-it-yourself point of view, the main provisos are that:
■ There must be·a *double check valve* or similar approved device fitted in the supply pipe to guard against contamination of the mains.
■ The supply pipe must have its own stopvalve and draincock fitted inside the house.
■ Underground supply pipes must be at least 750mm (30″) below ground level, and all fittings must be approved for underground use.

Another Byelaw states that you must inform your local water undertaking before going ahead with the job, if you pay water rates, this could mean you become liable for an extra *outside tap* or *standpipe* charge. But since interpretation of the other Byelaws can vary from area to area, you may also be required to have the finished installation inspected by a water authority official.

An outside tap is among the most useful of all plumbing additions – especially for the keen gardener.

OUTSIDE TAP OPTIONS

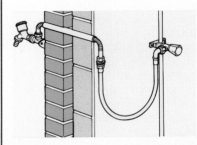

OPTION 1 – Fit an outside tap kit. These are convenient, but may not include all the parts you need – check before buying.

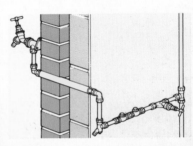

OPTION 2 – Make up your own kit. Buying the parts separately often works out cheaper and gives you more flexibility.

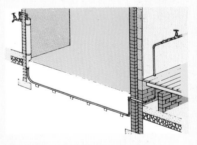

OPTION 3 – An underground supply. For a remote tape inside an outhouse, extend the pipe run underground with MDPE plastic pipe.

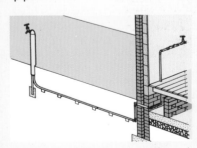

OPTION 4 – Fit a standpipe. This can be improvised from plastic rainwater pipe and screwed to an outhouse wall or left freestanding.

There are several parts options, depending on how you plan to do the job and on where the tap is being mounted. Usually it's best to draw a sketch plan and note down the parts as you go – refer to the illustrations and the instructions on the following pages for details.

Outside tap kits are available for both copper and polybutylene. As well as a tap, fixing plate and stopcock, most include some form of pipe connector. But many kits do not contain the double check valve now required by the Water Byelaws, and the break-in connectors found in some kits do not have universal approval when used on the rising main – check before you buy.

If you decide to buy the parts separately, you need:

A hose union bib tap, plus a 15mm×½" female iron *blackplate elbow* for mounting it on the wall; fix it with 38mm (1½") No. 8 brass screws.

A stopcock compression jointed for easy removal.

A draincock – you may be able to buy a stop/draincock combined.

A double check valve approved for use on rising mains.

A compression or soldered tee for branching off the rising main.

Elbows, bends, and 15mm pipe to make up the rest of the run. You also need a length of 22mm pipe to make a sleeve for the wall hole.

Tools checklist: Adjustable spanners or wrenches, junior hacksaw, electric drill and masonry bit, hired heavy duty masonry bit (eg 300×22mm) for drilling through the house wall, screwdrivers, cold chisel (maybe), flexible sealant, PTFE tape, blowlamp and heat proof mat (for soldered joints).

For an underground supply use *20mm MDPE* (medium density polyethylene) pipe, available in 25m (27yd) rolls. You also need:
■ A 15mm copper–20mm MDPE adapter coupling for the branch pipe, a length of 32mm (1¼") plastic waste for the hole sleeve, a 20mm to ½" female iron backplate elbow for connecting the tap, and 20mm elbow or other fittings approved for underground use.
■ 75mm (3") uPVC rainwater pipe, pipe clips, mineral fibre loose fill insulation and 1:3 repair mortar to make up a standpipe.

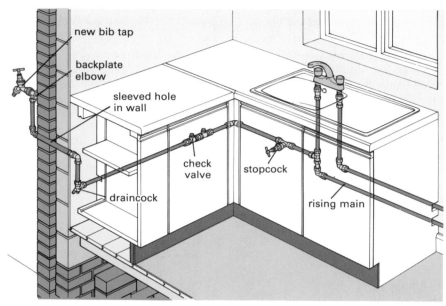

The standard outside tap arrangement – *a branch containing a stopcock, double check valve and draincock is taken off the rising main. From here, elbow fittings take the pipe through the house wall and down to a backplate elbow into which the tap is screwed. You have a choice of pipe materials (copper, stainless steel or polybutylene) and jointing methods.*

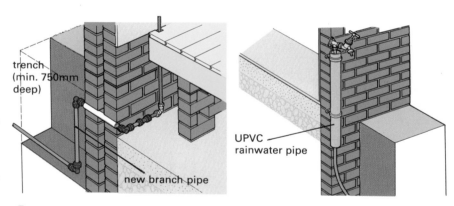

For a remote tap, *the pipe run from the house can be extended using 20mm MDPE pipe buried in a trench. The tap itself can be mounted on an outhouse wall, or on an improvised standpipe bedded in concrete.*

Trade tip

Neat and tidy

❛ *Conventional backplate elbows leave a length of pipe exposed, but fittings like the one shown from TOCOFLO allow the new tap to be mounted directly in front of the hole in the wall.*

Ensure that the tap ends up vertical when tightened into the backplate elbow. Pack it with tape, washers or sealant until it aligns, or use a self-locating bib tap like the Conex Snap Tap shown. ❜

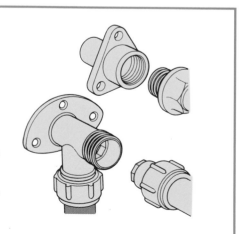

ARRANGING THE SUPPLY

The water supply for an outside tap must come from the rising main – not from a cold storage tank, where the pressure would be insufficient. The best place to break into the rising main is usually near the kitchen sink, where there is normally a branch with its own stopcock feeding the cold tap.

Other factors affecting your choice of break-in point include:
■ The tap position. If the tap is going on the house wall, it's best to site it over a gully. If you're fitting a remote tap, the pipe should leave the house below ground.
■ Obstructions on the wall. Make sure there are no downpipes or waste pipes at the point you plan to carry the pipe through the wall.
■ Access. You need room to work, and sufficient space to fit a stopcock, double check valve and drain cock before taking the pipe outside. Choosing a place where there is some free play in the rising main pipe will make it easier to fit a tee piece into the run.

In any event, try to keep the outside pipework to a bare minimum. Start the job by turning off the kitchen tap or main house stopcock and opening the kitchen cold tap to drain down the pipe.

The instructions here show how to run the pipe conventionally, using compression joints and copper pipe. If using plastic pipe, don't forget to continuity-bond the metal tap to the rest of the metal pipework using earthing straps and a length of single core earthing cable.

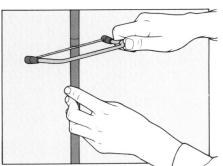

1 Having turned off the supply and drained down the rising main, cut squarely through the pipe at a convenient point using a junior hacksaw.

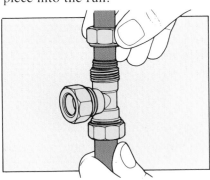

2 Mark and cut the pipe for a tee fitting, then prepare the pipe ends and fit the tee. (Use a slip tee or coupling if there is not enough free play in the pipe.)

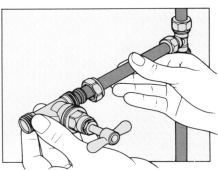

3 Run a short length of pipe from the tee and fit a stopcock in an accessible place. Check the arrow on the stopcock is in the direction of flow.

4 Select a point to break through the wall. Drill through from the outside, at a mortar joint, using a hired heavy duty masonry bit.

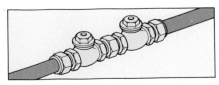

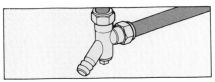

5 Add another short length of pipe and fit a double check valve. Continue the run using elbows where required and fit a drain cock at the lowest point.

Trade tip

Using a sleeve

❝ Cut a length of 22mm pipe to use as a sleeve and drive it through the hole in the wall. After completing the pipe run, seal inside and out with mastic. ❞

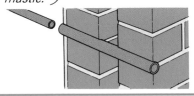

FITTING THE TAP

1 Measure and cut a length of pipe to pass through the wall, then fit an elbow, connecting length and backplate elbow. Mark the fixings.

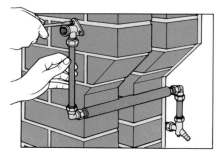

2 Drill and plug the wall, then complete the pipe run from inside the house. Returning outside, screw the backplate elbow firmly in place.

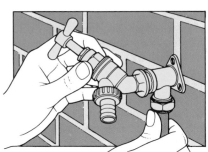

3 Wrap PTFE tape at least five times round the tap thread and screw it into the backplate. Tighten and set it vertical using a spanner on the body nut.

13

RUNNING AN UNDERGROUND SUPPLY

For an underground supply, the MDPE pipe should be connected inside the house, after the drain cock, and then passed through the house wall directly into the trench. If this is impossible to arrange, carry the pipe out at the lowest possible point, then run the exposed section in 75mm (3″) rainwater pipe packed with insulation material (see right).

MDPE is too thick to use 22mm copper pipe as a sleeve, so line the hole with a length of 32mm (1¼″) waste pipe instead. Use a long cold chisel or plugging chisel to enlarge the original drilled hole to the correct size.

Work out a route for the pipe, avoiding any obstructions. At the minimum specified trench depth of 750mm (30″) you are most unlikely to encounter gas or electricity pipes, but there may well be a drain – note the positions of nearby gullies and manholes to check. You'll need to fit elbows where the MDPE passes through the wall to avoid kinking, but otherwise you should aim to run the underground section in a single continuous length. See Problem Solver below for how to deal with obstructions such as a path.

After laying the pipe and connecting the far end, leave the trench uncovered until the installation has been inspected.

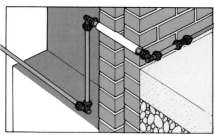

1 Connect the MDPE to the branch supply at its lowest point using a special coupling – plastic Philmac with green insert or compression with steel sleeve.

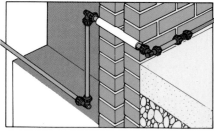

2 Sleeve the wall hole with plastic waste pipe. Carry the MDPE into the trench via an elbow fitting, then seal around the sleeve with mastic.

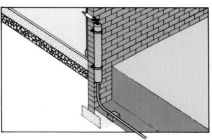

3 Run the pipe along the bottom of the trench in a continuous length, supported on bricks. At an outhouse, carry it inside, or fit a standpipe.

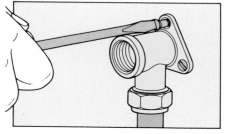

4 Use a 20mm backplate elbow to make the final tap connection. The elbow can be screwed to the wall or bedded in mortar in the top of the pipe.

MAKING A STANDPIPE

A standpipe of MDPE needs supporting. If there is a wall or wooden post to hand, run the MDPE through a length of 75mm (3″) uPVC rainwater pipe packed with mineral fibre loose fill insulation. Fix the rainwater pipe in place with pipe clips and screw the backplate elbow to the wall.

Alternatively, make up a support pipe as shown below, using a length of iron or steel pipe bedded in concrete. Tape the MDPE to the iron pipe, slip the rainwater pipe over the top, then pack with insulation.

In both cases, after fitting the tap pack the top 100mm (4″) of the standpipe with a strong mortar mix and shape it into a dome to deflect rain.

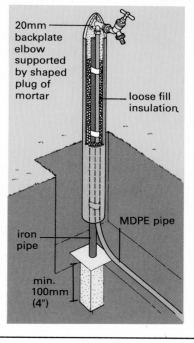

20mm backplate elbow supported by shaped plug of mortar

loose fill insulation

MDPE pipe

iron pipe

min. 100mm (4″)

PROBLEM SOLVER

Clearing obstructions

Obstructions such as paths and drives are sometimes difficult to avoid when running an underground pipe. A method used by many professionals is to drive a 1″ steel pipe or scaffold tube underneath the obstruction, then thread the MDPE through this. It takes a fair degree of skill to drive pipe long distances, but anything up to 1m (1yd) should present few problems.
■ Make certain that there are no drain pipes in the way.
■ Prepare the trench on either side of the obstruction.
■ Block the end of the sleeving pipe with a wedge of wood.
■ Set the pipe in the trench, supported on bricks. Check that it is level, and pointing in the right direction.
■ Tap the pipe into the ground with a club hammer to get it started, then stand beside the trench and switch to a sledge hammer to drive it home.

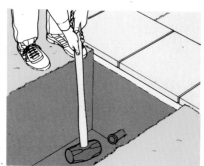

Drive a steel pipe under obstructions to act as a sleeve for the MDPE pipework.

MIXING CONCRETE AND MORTAR

Concrete and mortar are the builder's foremost raw materials.

Concrete – which is a mixture of cement, sand, gravel and water – is a building material in its own right, invaluable for patios, driveways, solid floors, and countless repair jobs around the home.

Mortar, which is concrete minus the gravel, is the builder's 'glue' that sticks together the bricks and blocks. It also gives a smooth finish to a floor and forms the hard, water-resistant coating found on many house walls (where it's usually called render).

Both are easy to mix by hand in the sort of quantities needed for most DIY jobs. The secret is to get the various ingredients in their correct proportions.

For larger jobs like building a house wall or laying a drive, hand mixing isn't practical because of the sheer bulk of material involved. It's better to hire a mechanical mixer, or, in the case of concrete, have it delivered ready mixed. Both these topics are covered later.

The ingredients explained

Cement is the binding agent in all concrete and mortar mixes. Made from powdered limestone and clay, it sets by chemical reaction when mixed with water. The most common type is *Ordinary Portland cement*, which is light grey in colour and can be used for virtually any job.

You may also come across *White Portland Cement,* which is used for coloured concrete, and *Masonry Cement,* which contains additives that make it easier to work when used in bricklaying mortar.

Quick setting ('Prompt') cement is a special type which sets in only a few minutes. It is sometimes used neat for small repair jobs.

Sand for concrete and mortar falls into two main categories:

Soft (Builder's) sand has small, rounded particles which make a mix smooth and easy to work but structurally weak. It often contains impurities such as clay dust, and is only used for bricklaying mortar.

Sharp sand has coarser, more angular particles which produce a stronger mix with greater 'grip'. *Concreting* sharp sand is coarse and relatively impure. *Fine washed* sharp sand has finer particles and is washed to remove all impurities. Use this type for rendering and screeding.

Coarse aggregate is the gravel or crushed stone which gives concrete its strength and bulk. It is sieved and then graded according to the size of the largest particles. Unless otherwise instructed, always specify '20mm' (¾") aggregate, which contains particles up to 20mm across.

Combined aggregate, commonly known as *all-in ballast*, is sand and coarse aggregate mixed together in the proportions required for concrete. Like aggregate it's sold by the particle size, so ask for '20mm (¾") all-in ballast' when ordering.

All-in ballast is more convenient to buy and use, which makes it popular among do-it-yourselfers. However, the proportions are never guaranteed, so it shouldn't be used for jobs where the exact ratio of sand to coarse aggregate is critical.

Mixing by hand is easy if the quantities are small.

Trade tip

Keep cement dry

❝ Keep bags of cement dry and off the ground – I put them on an old door or planks raised on bricks and cover them with a plastic sheet.

Left-over cement keeps for a few weeks stored in a bin liner sealed with a wire twist. ❞

MIXING TECHNIQUES

Hand-mixing mortar and concrete calls for virtually the same technique. The idea is to contain the mixing water with the dry ingredients so that it doesn't slop all over the place.

For very small quantities you can do the mixing with a pointing or bricklayer's trowel. For larger amounts, use a shovel or spade.

Always measure out the cement and the sand/aggregate in separate buckets – robust building buckets are available cheaply from builder's merchants. A watering can is ideal for adding the water, since it allows you to control the quantity accurately – avoid adding too much.

If the mix starts to harden while you're working with it, discard it and mix a fresh batch. Similarly, scrape the mixing area clean after every batch – the remnants of one can contaminate the next.

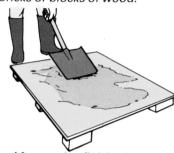

Trade tip
Keep it clean

❛ You can mix concrete and mortar on a path, patio or any clean hard-standing area, but this leaves you with the problem of cleaning up afterwards.

Where possible, I prefer to use a piece of board or an old flush door raised off the ground on bricks or blocks of wood.

After you've finished mixing, make a point of washing down the buckets, shovel and mixing board with clean water: if you let the mortar harden on them they'll be ruined. ❜

1 Measure out the cement in one bucket and the sand/aggregate in another. Turn the ingredients over slightly until the mixture is uniform in colour.

2 Gather the mixture into a volcano-shaped heap and form a well in the top. Pour in some of mixing water, taking care not to let it run out over the edges.

3 Shovel the dry mixture around the edge of the well into the water. When the water disappears, form a new well in the middle of the heap and repeat.

4 As the mixture starts to combine, add the water more carefully – normally, you need just enough to hold the dry ingredients together.

5 Finish by raking over the mixture as shown to check for unmixed pockets. Now check the consistency of the mix as described below.

PROBLEM SOLVER
Getting the mix right

The most difficult thing about mixing concrete and mortar is knowing how much water to add. Since sand and aggregate usually contain a fair amount of water when you buy them, it's hard to specify exact proportions.

Mortar for rendering and screeding is normally mixed fairly dry, so that the dry ingredients are *just* bound together. Otherwise, add enough water to make the mixture smooth and slippery – but not so much that it starts to run out.

The most effective test is to chop through the mix with your spade or shovel as shown to see how it holds its shape.

Mix too wet – water is gathering in the hollows.

Mix too dry – the ridges crumble as soon as they're formed.

Trade tip
Mix too wet

❛ I stiffen up a wet mix by adding a handful of dry cement and working it in quickly with the shovel. The trick is to sprinkle the cement lightly, so it doesn't form lumps. ❜

MIXES FOR DIFFERENT JOBS

The strength and working characteristics of concrete and mortar can be varied to suit the job in hand simply by altering the proportions of the ingredients. In the building industry, this process has been developed into an exact science. But for DIY mixing in small batches, the range of mixes described below will cover you for most jobs.

Buying the materials

The most convenient way to buy very small amounts of concreting materials is in dry-mixed bags – available from superstores, hardware stores and builder's merchants. These contain the cement, sand (and for concrete, aggregate) in the correct proportions, so all you need do is mix them with water.

Various mixtures are available in dry-mixed form, corresponding roughly to the mixes specified below. Bag sizes vary from brand to brand, but 2.5kg (6½lb), 5kg (11lb), 10kg (22lb), 15kg (33lb), 25kg (55lb) and 50kg (110lb) are commonly available.

For larger amounts, it's much more economical to buy the materials separately in bags from a builder's merchant. They are extremely heavy though, so try to find a supplier who will deliver.

Cement comes in 50kg (110lb) and (occasionally) 25kg (55lb) bags. Because it is the most costly concreting material, and doesn't keep well, all the mixes below are described in terms of how much cement they contain – 'one bag makes so-and-so', and so on.

Sand and aggregate come in 40-50kg (88-110lb) bags, but the exact quantity depends on how much water is present and is never guaranteed. The same applies to: **All-in ballast**, which is often available in smaller bag sizes too.

Volume versus weight

The proportions for concrete mixes are worked out by volume. An easy way to measure them is by the bucketful – so a 1:3 mix is one bucket of cement to three of sand.

But bagged materials are sold by weight. For any given volume, sand is about 10% heavier than cement and aggregate, and all-in ballast is about 30% heavier.

The mixes below give proportions by volume for each ingredient (with the concrete mixes use **either** sand and aggregate **or** all-in ballast). They also give the weight of sand/aggregate or ballast required for every 50kg of cement.

BRICKLAYING MORTAR MIX

Used for building exterior house walls, internal walls and extensions. Plasticizer (see overleaf) makes it easier to work.
By the 50kg bag of cement – enough for roughly 500 bricks or 300 screen blocks.
By the bucket of cement – enough for about 175 bricks or 105 screen blocks.
Dry-mix equivalent: Bricklaying Mortar mix

Cement	1 part	50kg
Soft sand	6 parts	330kg

STRONG MORTAR MIX

Stronger version of bricklaying mix, used for laying single-thickness garden walls and repair jobs to masonry. Adding PVA adhesive (see overleaf) makes it 'stickier', providing extra grip for small repairs.
By the 50kg bag of cement – enough for around 285 bricks, 170 screen blocks.
By the bucket of cement – enough for about 100 bricks, 60 screen blocks.
Dry-mix equivalent: Repair Mortar mix

Cement	1 part	50kg
Soft sand	3 parts	165kg

RENDERING MORTAR MIX

Used to repair rendered walls and as a final surface (screed) for solid concrete floors. Adding plasticizer makes it easier to work; adding PVA adhesive improves adhesion on small repair jobs.
By the 50kg bag of cement – enough to render an area of 23 sq m (28 sq yd) to an average thickness of 12mm (½"); enough to screed a floor area of 11.5 sq m (14 sq yd) to a depth of 25mm (1").
By the bucket of cement – enough to repair 8 sq m (9.75 sq yd) of 12mm (½") render or 4 sq m (5 sq yd) of 25mm (1") floor screed.
Dry-mix equivalent: Exterior Render or Sand/Cement

Cement	1 part	50kg
Sharp fine washed sand	6 parts	330kg

PAVING CONCRETE MIX

A strong concrete mix, used for concreting areas exposed to the elements – paths, garden steps and driveways.

By the 50kg bag of cement – enough to lay 1.2 sq m (1.4 sq yd) to a depth of 100mm (4″).

By the bucket of cement – would lay around 0.4 sq m to a depth of 100mm (4 sq ft/4″), but normally only used in larger quantities.

Dry-mix equivalent: No direct equivalent

Cement	1 part	50kg
Sharp concreting sand	1½ parts	80kg
Coarse aggregate	2½ parts	120kg
OR: All-in ballast	3½ parts	230kg

GENERAL-PURPOSE CONCRETE MIX

Suitable for all concreting jobs apart from exposed areas and foundations.

By the 50kg bag of cement – enough to lay a slab measuring 1220 × 1220mm (4 × 4′) to a thickness of 100mm (4″).

By the bucket of cement – enough to repair a patch of concrete measuring about a metre square (39 × 39″) to an average depth of 50mm (2″).

Dry-mix equivalent: Fine concrete mix

Cement	1 part	50kg
Sharp concreting sand	2 parts	110kg
Coarse aggregate	3 parts	140kg
OR: All-in ballast	4 parts	260kg

FOUNDATION CONCRETE MIX

The low cement content of this mix reduces the chances of cracking due to movement. Use it for all unexposed foundations – paved paths and patios, footings for garden walls, fence posts and washing line standards.

By the 50kg bag of cement – enough to fill 2m (6′) of trench measuring 300mm (12″) wide by 300mm (12″) deep.

By the bucket of cement – enough to bed 4 fence posts.

Dry-mix equivalent: Coarse concrete mix

Cement	1 part	50kg
Sharp concreting sand	2½ parts	140kg
Coarse aggregate	3½ parts	165kg
OR: All-in ballast	5 parts	325kg

ADDITIVES FOR CONCRETE AND MORTAR

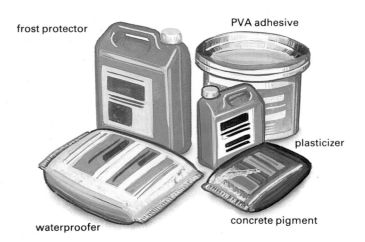

frost protector

PVA adhesive

plasticizer

waterproofer

concrete pigment

Plasticizer makes mortar mixes more elastic and easier to work. It is sold in plastic containers, and should be added to the mix strictly according to the maker's instructions.

PVA adhesive improves the adhesion of mortar used for repair jobs. Dilute it with 5-6 parts water and add to the water used for the mix.

Waterproofer seals up the open pores of mortar, increasing its weather resistance. Use when repointing and rendering.

Frost protector guards against frost damage to concrete while it is setting. Use for any concreting job if frost is expected.

Coloured pigments come in powder form, for mixing into concrete made with white cement. Various colours are available, but their effect is unpredictable and it's almost impossible to get an even colour when mixing in small batches.

LARGE SCALE CONCRETING

Although hand mixing concrete is fine for small-scale DIY jobs like bedding fence posts or casting a shed base, on larger concreting jobs it is seldom practical. Mixing large quantities of concrete by hand is extremely hard, heavy work. It is also unreliable – you may not be able to get the proportions of ingredients the same between batches – and if you don't work fast, there's a risk the concrete will start to set before you lay it.

One alternative is to hire a powered mixer. This is a good option for medium-sized jobs such as a larger slab or small driveway, but is still very hard work since the materials must all be shifted by hand several times.

On big projects such as a large driveway, a solid floor slab or foundations for an extension, a much better solution is to have the concrete delivered to the site ready mixed. This isn't normally an option on smaller jobs since many contractors will not deliver – or will put a hefty surcharge on – loads of less than about 6 cu m; enough to lay a 10×4m (30×12') drive 150mm (6") thick. Even so, it pays to check your local Yellow Pages: some companies specializing in the DIY market will supply much smaller quantities using special mixer lorries, while others mix the concrete on the spot so that you only pay for what you use.

GETTING READY

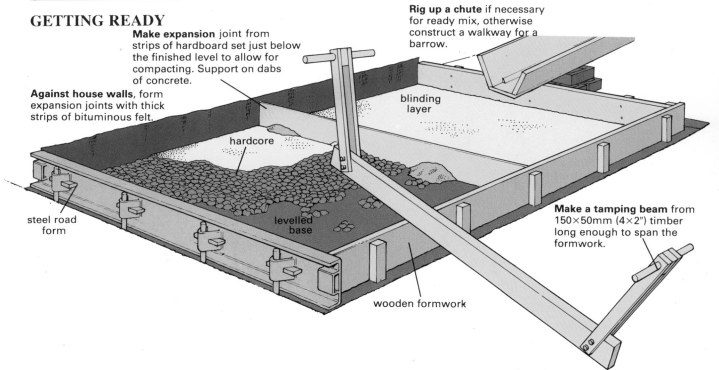

Make expansion joint from strips of hardboard set just below the finished level to allow for compacting. Support on dabs of concrete.

Against house walls, form expansion joints with thick strips of bituminous felt.

Rig up a chute if necessary for ready mix, otherwise construct a walkway for a barrow.

blinding layer

hardcore

levelled base

steel road form

wooden formwork

Make a tamping beam from 150×50mm (4×2") timber long enough to span the formwork.

If you use ready mix it is essential that everything is ready in advance; the concrete must be poured and finished within 2–4 hours. And even when mixing your own, it is a good idea to get the site ready before buying the materials.

Level the area and lay any hardcore, then put up formwork to contain the concrete. This can be made from timber, but for a large slab you may find it is worth hiring steel *road forms* which are easier to use. The standard length is 3m (10') and they come in different depths from 100mm (4") up.

Tools and other materials are much the same as needed for laying a small slab, although it is worth making a proper *tamping beam*. If you are using ready mix it may also be worth rigging up a chute so the concrete can be discharged straight on to the site.

Expansion joints are important on large areas such as a drive or path to prevent the concrete from cracking. Divide the site with thin strips of wood (or even hardboard) at intervals depending on its size (see table), then lay the concrete in separate bays.

RECOMMENDED JOINT INTERVALS

Concrete thickness	Width of site* up to 1m	1–2m	2–4m
75mm	every 2m	every 2.5m	every 3m
100mm	—	every 2–3m	every 4m
150mm	—	every 3–4m	every 4m

* Sites over 4m wide must be divided into bays of equal width.

Trade tip
Buying materials

❝Bear in mind that large quantities of cement, sand and ballast are bulky and heavy, so you need somewhere to store them until they can be used. Cement must be stored off the ground and under cover; it will be ruined if it becomes wet. Sand and ballast are normally tipped loose off the back of a lorry, so it helps if there is access near to the site. Keep the sand dry; it becomes very heavy when wet and makes mixing harder.

If materials must be carried through the house, you can either order them bagged (more expensive) or use a barrow.❞

USING A MIXER

Hired concrete mixers are commonly electric powered, but diesel and petrol versions are also available.

The type often stocked for DIY use is known as a *4/3 barrow* or *½ bag size*. These are fairly lightweight and can be carried by an estate car or small van; they make 0.08 cu m (3 cu ft) per mix. *5/3 ½* models are harder to transport and manoeuvre on site, but worth considering for big jobs. They make 0.09 cu m (3½ cu ft).

Use a mixer in this order:
- Put in half the gravel, then half the water, then all the sand.
- Mix briefly. Add all the cement then the rest of the gravel.
- Slowly add enough water so that the concrete comes cleanly off the blades of the mixer – it should not be allowed to become sloppy.
- Mix for about two minutes.
- Clean the mixer whenever you stop work for any length of time; the easy way is to leave it running with some gravel and water in the drum.

Mixer safety

- Keep the lead off the ground.
- Do not overload the drum.
- Keep children well away.
- Do not look into the drum, reach in, or put in a shovel while the mixer is running.

1 Chock the mixer near the site with its lead well out of the way. Make sure it is stable and try to set it high enough to tip straight into your barrow.

2 Put in half the gravel with half the water and all the sand. Run for a short time, then add the cement and the rest of the gravel.

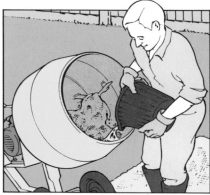

3 Slowly add water to the mix until the concrete clings together and falls cleanly away from the mixer blades. Do not let it become sloppy.

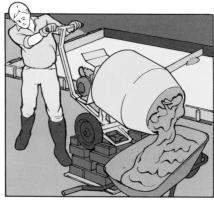

4 Tip the concrete out of the mixer drum and into your barrow to transfer it to the site. Alternatively, tip it on to a board and shovel it up.

USING READY MIX

Before ordering ready mix, think about access. The best place for the load to be discharged is straight on to the site, but the mixer lorry will be wide and heavy and it may not be possible to bring it within reach of the short chute fitted at the back. If you cannot rig up an extension chute to a suitable access point, the concrete must be discharged as near to the site as possible then transferred by barrow.

In this case, remember that concrete must not be dumped on the road or pavement without the agreement of the local authority. You will also need a lot of help – a cubic metre of concrete fills about 25 barrow loads – if the concrete is to be transferred and laid before it starts to set.

Get two or three quotes before ordering, being sure to state what mix you require (see right). You should also sort out where the concrete is to be discharged, and agree a

Ready mix is best discharged straight on to the site.

delivery time; avoid rush hours in case the lorry is held up.

The type of mix is normally specified by quoting a British Standard number and one or two pieces of technical jargon. For practical purposes there are three:

General purpose mix for most jobs except foundations and exposed paving Ask for *C20P to BS 5328* and specify *medium to high workability* with a 20mm maximum aggregate.

Foundation mix for foundations, footings and a base under paving slabs. Ask for *C7.5P to BS5328* and specify *high workability with a 20mm maximum aggregate*.

Paving mix for exposed paving such as drives. Ask for a *Special Prescribed Mix* and specify *minimum cement content 330kg per cu m, 4% entrained air, target slump 75mm*.

LEVELLING A SITE

One of the most basic and important parts of many outdoor construction projects is to provide a flat, level concrete base – possibly for a patio or carport, or as a firm foundation for a shed or greenhouse.

Time spent getting the site correctly marked out, excavated and levelled makes the job of pouring and smoothing the concrete very much easier. It also helps to ensure that the finished base doesn't crack or suffer from drainage problems.

Levelling a site is not a difficult job and you're unlikely to need any special tools – a tape measure, spirit level, garden spade, timber straightedge, string and a supply of sturdy wooden pegs (plus a mallet to drive them in) are sufficient.

Site levelling – the first stage of most outdoor concreting jobs.

CHECKING YOUR SITE

First look for obvious obstructions (see Problem Solver).

If there's a slope, plan how to deal with it – there's no need to measure it yet, but unless the slope is very slight the site must be levelled.

If the slab is going next to the house, it must be at least 150mm (6″) below the damp-proof course (DPC). On a sloping site, this in turn may affect the way you deal with access from the house, surface water run-off and buried services.

A flat site or gentle slope needs only minimal levelling work.

A slope up from the house causes water to run on to the site.

A slope down helps water run-off, but watch for buried services.

A crossways or combination slope may create access problems.

DEALING WITH SLOPES

Option 1: Cut in Excavate into the slope to create a level base, and construct retaining walls to hold back the garden. The main problem is the natural drainage of ground water from the slope down towards the site. And if the ground slopes away from the house, cutting in may mean that the slab ends up too far down or interferes with services.

Option 2: Build up The alternative to excavation is to extend up above the line of the slope by building a retaining wall and then backfilling behind it. This may require a lot of filling material, and it can be tricky to pack the backfill thoroughly enough to prevent subsidence. Drainage of surface water is easy to control.

Option 3: Cut in and build up This is a useful solution because what is excavated from one part can be used to fill the other. It works well on sites that slope in more than one direction, and on steep slopes it can be used to create a series of terraces. Drainage off the slope may still be a problem on the excavated part.

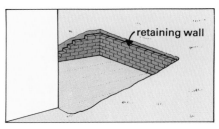
On upward slopes cutting in means building a retaining wall and arranging drainage for the water.

Downward slopes can be built up behind a retaining wall but you need plenty of infill material.

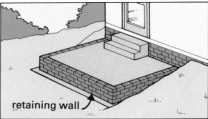
Part-excavation provides its own infill and does not change the level so much as other options.

SETTING OUT AND EXCAVATING

Level ground, and slopes with only a slight fall in one or both directions (up to around 300mm [1'] from side to side), are marked out in the same way. For how to deal with steeper slopes, see opposite.

To check the fall, drive in a short peg at the 'top' side of the site and a longer one at the bottom. Run a string line from the base of the short peg to the long peg and use a spirit level to check when it's horizontal. Then tie the string to the long peg and measure the distance from the knot to the ground.

Check the fall of a slope with pegs top and bottom. Stretch a string from the base of the 'top' peg, set it level, then measure where it strikes the bottom peg.

Mark the site out (right) with string lines and clear away the soil ready for accurate levelling.

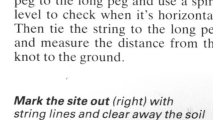

PREPARING LEVEL GROUND

Marking out a level site is quite straightforward – and even if the area has a slight slope, this won't affect the first stages of the excavation:

■ Mark out the area of the site and clear the ground of turf or plants.
■ Remove usable topsoil for later use or transfer it to other parts of the garden.
■ Excavate the base to roughly the right depth all over. It is then ready to be levelled accurately (see opposite).

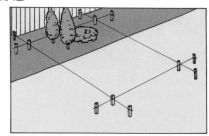

1 Mark the corners of the site with pegs. Then set up string lines between pegs driven in well outside the area so that lines tied between them cross at each corner peg.

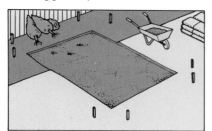

2 Remove the corner pegs and lines so you don't fall over them. Remove turf or vegetation and skim off the topsoil with your spade for later use or disposal around the garden.

3 Replace the four string lines and make spade cuts round the site. Remove the lines again and dig out the subsoil roughly level to about 150mm (6") below the lowest point of the slope.

Trade tip

No strings attached

❝ Removable string lines run between pegs set outside the area allow you to work unimpeded – simply reposition them when you need to check the accuracy of the excavation. I drive in a nail near the top of each peg so I can wind the string on and off. ❞

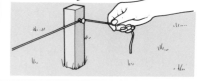

PREPARING A SLOPE

The method to use depends on which levelling option you have chosen. Use your string lines to mark out the rough level as well as the extent of the area:

Option 1: Cut in Set up the lines on the surface of the slope and start excavating from the downhill side, creating a roughly level platform as you work. At the uphill side of the excavation, cut back far enough to allow for foundations for the retaining wall. Slope the sides of the excavation to prevent them falling in – you can backfill behind the wall later.

Option 2: Build up Build the retaining wall first, then fill in behind it later. Mark out the site and use your string lines as a guide to dig trenches for the wall foundations. You need to allow at least a week after building the wall before you attempt to add

the infill, in case you disturb the mortar before it has set.

Option 3: Cut in and build up This is a compromise between the techniques used in Options 1 and 2. Build any retaining walls in the same way as Option 2. When the mortar has set, excavate the material from the high side as in Option 1 and use it to fill in the area behind the wall, packing it down firmly.

On an uphill slope, excavate back far enough to build your retaining wall. Backfill later.

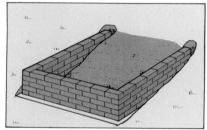
On a downhill slope, build your retaining wall before adding the infill material.

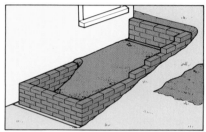
Move the earth over to create new levels and provide space to build retaining walls.

GETTING ACCURATE LEVELS

With your site excavated and roughly levelled, the next stage is to level it accurately ready for concreting. This is done by fixing the height at one point and then taking all other levels from here.

Drive in a stout wooden stake – called a *datum peg* – just outside one corner of the site, so that the top of the peg is at the same height as the finished level of the slab.

Note that if the slab joins on to a wall of the house, the top of the datum peg must be at least 150mm (6″) below the damp-proof course (DPC) to avoid damp problems. If you can't see the DPC, assume it's the same height as the doorstep.

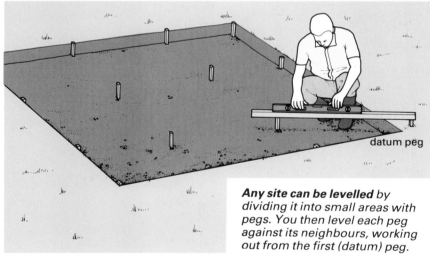

Any site can be levelled by dividing it into small areas with pegs. You then level each peg against its neighbours, working out from the first (datum) peg.

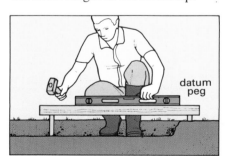
1 Drive in a datum peg and drive others at about 1m intervals across the site. Level the peg nearest to the datum using a straightedge and spirit level.

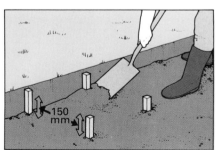
2 Level the other pegs in turn against their neighbours. Then dig out or replace subsoil until all the pegs protrude from the ground by the same amount.

3 If you want a fall across the finished slab, set each peg a little below the last by using a block or screw to prop up one end of the straightedge.

Dealing with obstructions

Obvious on-site obstacles include manholes and gullies (see below), and mature trees which must either be felled or built around.

Even if nothing shows on the surface, be aware that there may be underground drain runs, water and gas pipes, and electricity cables. Although these should be below the depth of an excavation on a level site, they are within the depth you might reach when cutting into a slope. Damaging any of these services (see right) could be expensive – fatal in the case of power cables.

The position of manholes can give clues to drain runs. Water supply pipes usually run in a straight line from the point at which they enter the house to the water authority's main stopcock. Underground cables could run anywhere; a circuit running from the house to an outbuilding should be easier to locate.

All of these services need to be rerouted to avoid your site. Altering drains requires local authority approval and all work on mains pipes/cables must be left to the authority concerned. It may be less trouble to rethink the excavation.

Manholes

If a manhole falls within the planned excavation, you need to dig round it carefully. You may also have to raise the sides of the chamber so that the cover finishes flush with the surface of the new concrete. (This is a good opportunity to fit a new, better-looking cover and frame.)

On sloping sites, a manhole may influence the way you decide to level the slope, and what height you work to.

Gullies

Open gullies taking downstairs waste pipes, and existing yard gullies that come within the area of a new slab may also have to be built up. Old-style gullies of brick and concrete *benching* normally have to be broken up and reconstructed. Clay and plastic gullies can usually simply be fitted with extension pieces to raise the grid level.

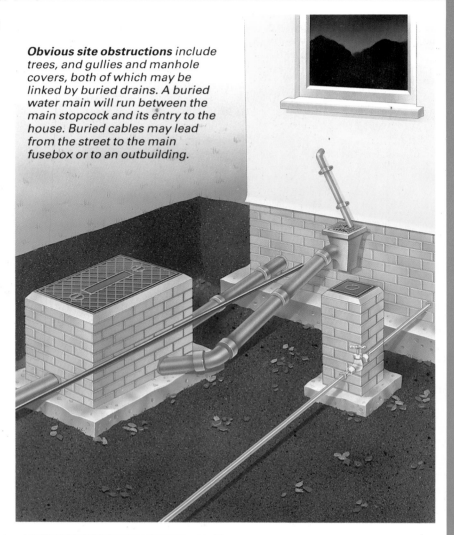

Obvious site obstructions include trees, and gullies and manhole covers, both of which may be linked by buried drains. A buried water main will run between the main stopcock and its entry to the house. Buried cables may lead from the street to the main fusebox or to an outbuilding.

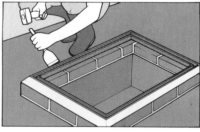

1 Raise the manhole cover and prise off the metal frame in which it sits – don't let rubble fall in the drain. Then build up the chamber walls with bricks.

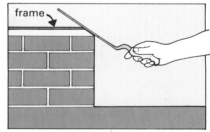

2 Set the frame (or a new frame) at the same height as the finished level of the slab. Bed it on mortar, taking care none falls in the drain.

On old brick and concrete gullies, demolish the masonry and build up a new gully to the level of the concrete slab you are proposing to build.

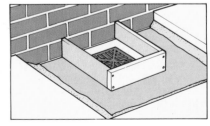

On newer style clay or plastic gullies, simply leave the grid in place. Make a temporary wooden frame to fit the top and cast the slab around it.

LAYING A CONCRETE SLAB

A concrete slab makes a strong, long-lasting base for any number of garden constructions, including sheds, barbecues and paved patios. And so long as the area isn't too large, it's a job which two people can complete in a weekend.

The method covered here is suitable for laying a small area of concrete – up to around 3m (9') square – on a site which you have already prepared and levelled. It assumes you intend to mix the concrete by hand.

For larger areas, such as a driveway, hand mixing isn't really practical and you should either hire a concrete mixer or get the concrete delivered ready mixed.

A concrete slab provides the base for this attractive greenhouse.

WHAT THICKNESS?

	Hardcore	Concrete
Base only	50mm (2")	75mm (3")
Exposed or floor slab	50mm (2")	100mm (4")

If subsoil is poorly drained, loose or clay, increase thicknesses by 25mm (1").

HOW MUCH CONCRETE?

Find the length and width of your proposed slab in **metres** and multiply them together. Using a calculator, multiply the result by:

   .075 for a 75mm thickness
   .100 for a 100mm thickness
   .125 for a 125mm thickness

to find the volume in **cubic metres**. **Now check the chart below** (showing cubic metres of concrete per 50kg bag of cement) to find out what weight of materials to buy for your chosen concrete mix. Round up to the next whole bag of cement, to allow for wastage.

.... Shopping List ....

Concrete Use a *general purpose* mix if the slab is to form the base for an outbuilding that has its own floor; use a *paving mix* for a hardstanding or barbecue base, or when the slab itself will form the floor. Check the tables for what thickness to use (left) and what weight of materials to buy (below). Add an extra bag of sand to spread over the hardcore.

Hardcore for the base can be broken brick, rubble or concrete – but not plaster. If you don't have any suitable material to hand, it can be ordered from a builder's merchant and delivered.

Timber boards (*formwork*) are essential for casting the slab. For a small slab you need four boards, each a bit longer than the slab dimensions (you will need more if you decide to cast the slab in bays – see overleaf). Ideally, the boards should be the same width as the combined depth of the hardcore and concrete (see table), and at least 25mm (1") thick. If they are wider, you have the extra job of recessing them into the ground.

Old floorboards from demolition yards make good formwork, otherwise buy sawn softwood boards from a timber merchant. They're not expensive, so make sure you have enough.

At the same time, get a dozen or so 300mm (1') lengths of sawn 50×25mm (2×1") softwood to make wooden support pegs. You also need a 150×50mm (6×2") plank 300mm (1') wider than the slab to use as a *tamping beam* for compacting and levelling the concrete.

Other materials: Nails, heavy duty polythene sheet.
Other tools: wheelbarrow (preferably builder's type), shovel or spade, rake, hose, two builder's buckets, sledge hammer, steel float, wooden float (optional), hammer, stiff broom.

GENERAL PURPOSE MIX: 1:2:3 cement/sand/aggregate OR 1:4 cement/all-in ballast   * 1 bag=50kg

	1 bag*	2 bags*	3 bags*	4 bags*	5 bags*	6 bags*	7 bags*	8 bags*	9 bags*	10 bags*
Cement	1 bag*	2 bags*	3 bags*	4 bags*	5 bags*	6 bags*	7 bags*	8 bags*	9 bags*	10 bags*
Sand	105kg	210kg	315kg	420kg	525kg	630kg	735kg	840kg	945kg	1050kg
Coarse aggregate	185kg	370kg	555kg	740kg	925kg	1110kg	1295kg	1480kg	1665kg	1850kg
All-in ballast	290kg	580kg	870kg	1160kg	1450kg	1740kg	2030kg	2320kg	2610kg	2900kg
...makes	0.15cu m	0.31cu m	0.47cu m	0.63cu m	0.78cu m	0.93cu m	1.09cu m	1.25cu m	1.4cu m	1.56cu m

PAVING MIX: 1:1½:2½ cement/sand/aggregate OR 1:3½ cement/all-in ballast   * 1 bag=50kg

	1 bag*	2 bags*	3 bags*	4 bags*	5 bags*	6 bags*	7 bags*	8 bags*	9 bags*	10 bags*
Cement	1 bag*	2 bags*	3 bags*	4 bags*	5 bags*	6 bags*	7 bags*	8 bags*	9 bags*	10 bags*
Sand	75kg	150kg	225kg	300kg	375kg	450kg	525kg	600kg	675kg	750kg
Coarse aggregate	150kg	300kg	450kg	600kg	750kg	900kg	1050kg	1200kg	1350kg	1500kg
All-in ballast	225kg	450kg	675kg	900kg	1125kg	1350kg	1575kg	1800kg	2025kg	2250kg
...makes	0.125cu m	0.25cu m	0.375cu m	0.5cu m	0.625cu m	0.75cu m	0.875cu m	1.00cu m	1.125cu m	1.25cu m

LAYING AND LEVELLING

Begin by excavating and levelling the site to accommodate the layers of hardcore and concrete (see right). Excavate a little further than the slab area to leave room for the formwork.

Work out where you're going to mix the concrete and how it can be transferred to the site. If there is no suitable area of hardstanding, clear a patch of bare ground and ram down the soil so that there's no chance of it contaminating the mix.

Have at least one helper. Organize things so that one of you mixes and ferries the concrete while the other pours and levels.

Below: the stages involved in laying a slab – building the formwork (1), casting (2), finishing (3) and curing (4).

Against a house wall (left), divide the site into bays with an extra formwork board. This allows you to cast and level one bay working from inside the other.

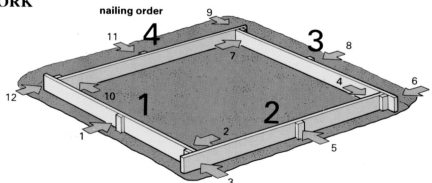

well rammed hardc[...]

formwork

excavated site

Trade tip

Clean away

❝ *When building formwork, smear the insides of the boards with cooking oil or old engine oil so that they'll part cleanly from the concrete when removed.* ❞

CONSTRUCTING FORMWORK

Avoid cutting boards by building up the formwork as shown (notice that each board is supported by at least two pegs to stop it tipping outwards). Nail the boards to the pegs and to each other using 50mm (2″) nails.

If the slab is against a house wall and access is restricted, fit extra boards to divide the slab into bays so that you can pour and level the concrete from inside the frame.

nailing order

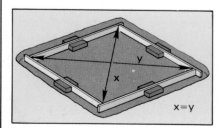

1 Prop the boards temporarily in the position shown above. Check they are square to each other by measuring the diagonals – which should be equal.

x = y

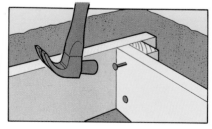

2 Drive in wooden pegs outside the boards at corners and at 1m (3′) intervals in between. Nail everything together following the sequence shown.

3 Using a spirit level check that the boards are more or less level. If necessary pack under them with soil or stones to adjust their heights.

LAYING THE HARDCORE

1 Shovel the hardcore into area bounded by the formwork and spread it evenly. Break up the larger pieces with a pick or sledge hammer.

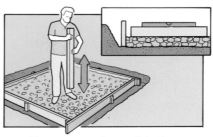

2 Use a stout piece of timber on end to ram the hardcore down firmly. Every so often, check that the layer is roughly level with a spirit level and batten.

3 Finish by shovelling a thin layer of sand or gravel over the base to fill any low spots. This makes the concrete easier to pour and level.

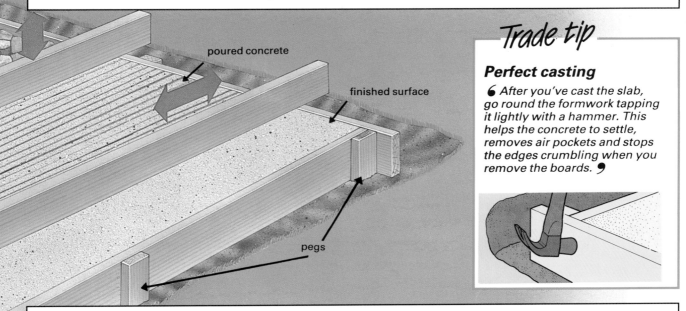

poured concrete

finished surface

pegs

Trade tip

Perfect casting

❝ After you've cast the slab, go round the formwork tapping it lightly with a hammer. This helps the concrete to settle, removes air pockets and stops the edges crumbling when you remove the boards. ❞

LAYING THE CONCRETE

As the tables on page 25 show, it takes a surprisingly large amount of concrete to fill even a small slab. Don't exhaust yourself trying to complete it all in one go: if you run out of steam, simply divide the site with an extra formwork board and a couple of pegs, then leave the rest until the next day. If you have to break off while mixing, discard what's left of the old batch before mixing another.

1 Unless you're mixing right next to the site, lay down a path of planks so that you can transfer barrowloads of concrete straight to where they're needed.

2 While one of you mixes and ferries the concrete, the other should use a garden rake to spread it roughly 25mm (1") above the tops of the formwork boards.

3 When the site is full, run the tamping beam up and down across the concrete to compact it. Fill any indents that appear, then repeat the process.

4 Now rest the tamping beam on top of the formwork boards and run it across the slab in a sawing motion to level it and remove excess concrete.

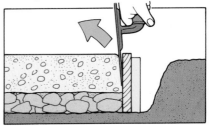

5 Finally, run the blade of a steel float right around the outside of the casting. Angle the blade inwards slightly, so that the edges are rounded off.

FINISHING AND CURING

Finishing By the time you've compacted and levelled the concrete, it should already be starting to dry. At this stage, think about what surface finish you want. If the slab is to form a floor, a smooth finish is probably best. Otherwise, give it one of the non-slip finishes shown right.

You can do the smoothing with a steel float, rather than a wooden one, but take care not to over-trowel: this causes cement and water to rise to the surface, creating a thin dusty layer which will crumble when it dries.

Curing Concrete has to be given time to set – a process known as *curing*. If it dries out too fast, it tends to crack. If you walk on it too soon, it breaks up around the edges.

Protect the slab by covering it with a sheet of thick polythene, weighted with bricks. You can knock away the formwork after 24 hours, but leave the slab covered for a further 7-8 days before building on it or exposing it to heavy loads.

For an exposed aggregate finish, spray the surface lightly with water as it hardens and brush away the cement and sand. Wash again a day later to clean up.

For a smooth finish, lightly run over the surface with a metal float in a circular motion. As the concrete hardens, give it a final polish with a steel float.

A brushed finish gives an even texture. Smooth the surface with a wooden float, then brush the slab lightly in a regular pattern using a stiff broom.

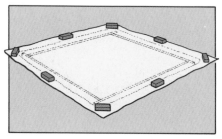

Cover the slab with a sheet of polythene to stop it drying out too quickly and to protect it from rain. Leave at least a day before removing the formwork.

PROBLEM SOLVER

Heavy weather

Extreme weather conditions can ruin a freshly cast slab, so be prepared to act immediately.

In a hot, dry spell, cover the slab with old blankets or sacking instead of polythene. Spray the covering with water twice a day to keep it moist while the concrete is curing.

Don't cast the slab if there's a frost. If frost is expected during the curing time, shovel a layer of sand or soil over the polythene to act as an insulating barrier. (It's not worth buying frost inhibitor additive for a small slab, since it will probably only be available in bulk sizes.)

Cover the slab with sacking and hose down regularly to stop it drying too fast in hot weather.

Shovel soil or sand over the polythene cover if frost is expected while the slab cures.

Trade tip

Surface defects

❝ If you notice any of the following defects as the concrete starts to harden, act fast to 'rescue' the slab:

Hollows in the surface show the concrete isn't properly compacted. Shovel in more concrete, re-tamp and re-level.

Surface break-up as you level the concrete suggest that the mix is too dry. Sprinkle with neat cement, spray lightly with water, and smooth with a float.

Liquid on the surface is a sign of over-trowelling. Work the liquid back into the slab by slicing the concrete at intervals with your float blade, then smooth out again quickly. Brush off any residue as the slab cures. ❞

DESIGNING A PAVED PATIO

A patio built from easy-to-lay paving slabs brings the world of barbecues, outdoor eating and relaxing in the sun quite literally to your door. At the same time it adds an extra dimension to the garden, and is a lot easier to keep up than a lawn or flower beds.

Laying a patio like this is a straightforward matter of bedding the slabs in dry sand over a firm base – either your existing paving, or a layer of compacted rubble. The work can be strenuous, since it involves excavating and lifting heavy weights, but it's not difficult and it doesn't require any special skills.

At the end, you'll have a surface that is more than strong enough to walk and sit on, and which should last for years. (The technique described here is not strong enough to make a drive or a car standing.)

The first stage of the job – designing your new patio – is also the most enjoyable. Working out what pattern you want and drawing up a scale plan can be fun, and is by far the most accurate way of estimating what materials you need. It also helps you decide what to do with fixed features like drains, manhole covers and trees before they become a problem.

Choosing the site

You may already have some sort of concrete or paved area next to the house, though the chances are this is too small, inconveniently placed or not very attractive. Possibly you can use it as a base for part of the new patio. But you don't *have* to build on the same spot – or even up against the house (though this may mean laying a path as well).

The areas to avoid are:
■ Steeply sloping ground. A patio next to the house must slope away from it 25mm in every metre for proper drainage. If the site slopes too much, you'll have to level it and build retaining walls.
■ Somewhere too much in the shade or exposed to the wind.
■ Areas containing fixed obstacles that have to be worked around.

CHOOSING THE SLABS

Paving slabs come in a variety of shapes, colours and sizes, giving you plenty of scope for creating attractive designs and patterns.

Slabs are cast from concrete and have smooth or textured surfaces. The more expensive type are made from a mixture containing crushed stone and often have a 'riven' surface like real stone.

The most common shapes are square, rectangular and hexagonal. You can get them as small as 220mm (9″) square, but the most popular sizes are 450mm (18″) square, 600 × 450mm (24 × 18″) and 600mm (24″) square. Bear in mind that the largest slabs can weigh up to 40kg (90lb) each, and are much harder to handle.

Half slabs are available for some ranges and are useful for filling in gaps; there is a special set for squaring off hexagonals. Ordinary slabs can be cut by hand but you're better hiring an angle grinder with a stone-cutting disc to cut riven slabs cleanly.

Square slabs can be laid in a regular grid (**A**) or a staggered pattern (**B**); rectangular slabs look better staggered, but if you're feeling ambitious you could experiment with basket weave (**C**) or herringbone patterns (**D**). Hexagonal slabs only fit together one way (**E**), but produce an interesting pattern on their own; use half slabs to square off.

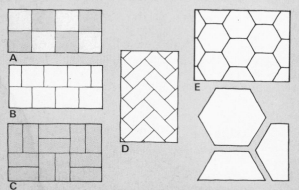

Top On a small patio, why not ring the changes? Here, a mixture of full slabs, half slabs and a gravelled-over centrepiece add plenty of visual interest.
Above Step out into the sun – having a patio adds a new dimension to your living space, not to mention the pleasure of eating and relaxing outdoors.

DRAWING A PLAN

The ideal basis for your plan is 5mm squared paper, taking each square as 150mm (6″). On this scale, a 450mm square slab takes up a 3×3 block of squares, while a 600×450mm slab uses a 4×3 block – there should be plenty of room on a single sheet.

You also need a sheet of tracing or greaseproof paper.

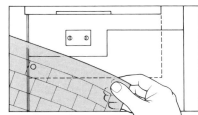

1 *Make a rough sketch of the site. Mark in the fixed points and obstacles, measuring their distances from each other and the boundaries of the area.*

2 *Draw the site showing all these features to scale on the squared paper. Rule in the slabs in pencil on the tracing paper and place it over the squares.*

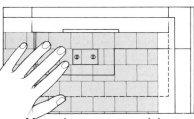

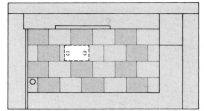

3 *Move the trace around the site plan to see where the slabs fit best. If there's an obstacle you need to minimize the number of slabs affected.*

4 *When you're satisfied, draw the site plan on the trace. Where you're leaving out slabs, rub them out. Ink in the others and shade in any pattern.*

Trade tip

A stitch in time

❛ *It's always a good idea to plan features you might want to put in later, even if you are not going to build them right away. If you're thinking about, say, a brick barbecue or planter, work out the dimensions and leave a space in units of whole and half slabs. This'll save a lot of lifting and cutting.* ❜

WORKING AROUND OBSTACLES

Your proposed site may include features such as a tree which you don't want to cut down, or a manhole cover or drain gully, neither of which can easily be moved. (It's also illegal to prevent access to a manhole). So these features need to be incorporated in the patio – in the case of a drain either by building it into the new surface, or by covering it in such a way that it's easily accessible (see Problem Solver).

If you are going to build the patio around an obstacle, adjust the slab layout to get as close as possible with whole or half slabs (see Drawing a Plan above). Around a tree, leave a space of at least one slab on each side.

Right Here, a manhole cover is surrounded by a cobbled area and disguised with a wheelbarrow.

PLANNING THE EXCAVATION

What you do with any existing paving or concrete on a site next to the house depends on one crucial factor – the height of the damp proof course (DPC). The picture opposite shows the most common types of DPC.

Look for rows of darker-than-normal engineering bricks **A**, a thin black line in the mortar **B** (or a wider-than-normal mortar joint), small circular vents (ceramic respirators) **C**, or blobs of mortar at regular intervals (indicating a chemical DPC) **D**. If you can't find any of these, take the DPC level as being directly below the height of the nearest sill or threshold.

The surface of the new patio must be at least 150mm (6″) below the DPC. If your existing paving or concrete is in good condition and at least 250mm (10″) below the DPC, you can lay the new patio over the top without a hardcore base. If it's closer to the DPC than this, it must be broken up and excavated.

You can hire a pickaxe to break up pavers or thin concrete yourself. For thicker concrete, employ a builder for the day to break it up, then use it as hardcore for the new foundations.

PROBLEM SOLVER

Dealing with drains

When excavating the site you'll need to leave about 150mm (6″) on each side of any drains undisturbed. If drainage gullies are against the side of the house, build around them. If there's a gully in the middle of the site, see the diagram on the right which shows how to maintain drainage. Manhole covers can be treated as shown on the right, or by building around them and raising the cover level with the new surface using a special extension fitting.

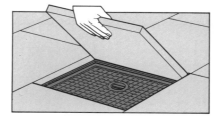

If you are building over a manhole cover, arrange your slabs so that as few as possible fall on top of it – use half slabs if necessary, to avoid having to lift too many for inspection.

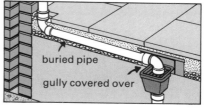

buried pipe

gully covered over

If there's a gully taking water off the roof, maintain this arrangement under the patio surface by running a length of plastic drain pipe from the downpipe to the gully grille.

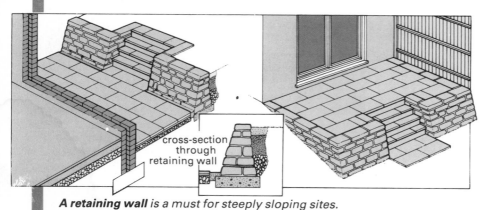

cross-section through retaining wall

A retaining wall is a must for steeply sloping sites.

Sloping sites

If the ground slopes sharply towards the house, you'll have to excavate the soil to level the site; you may also need to build retaining walls along the edge of the earth banks. If the site slopes away from the house, plan to build up the bank to produce a level surface, and construct a low retaining wall at the end of the site.

LAYING A PAVED PATIO

Having designed your new patio and drawn up a laying plan (see pages 29-32), you're ready to start work.

The illustrations overleaf show how the patio is constructed. Bedding the slabs 'dry' in sand means you don't have to worry about mixing huge quantities of concrete. Nor do you have to hire special compacting equipment, as you would for smaller paving blocks.

The slabs themselves can be laid directly on the dry sand, or on fist-sized blobs of mortar. The second method makes the slabs slightly easier to position, but is purely optional – it has no great effect on their stability.

The hardcore's purpose is to provide a firm base for the patio. It can consist of stones, bricks, and any *clean* builders' rubble, broken into pieces no larger than half a brick. If you have broken up an old paved area, this may provide enough suitable material.

First steps

Organize things well in advance. You'll be dealing with bulky, heavy materials, so make sure you have help and allow plenty of time.

Your laying plan (see pages 29-32) will tell you how many slabs to get; they're sold in DIY superstores, garden centres and builder's merchants. If possible, order the slabs along with all the other materials and have everything delivered at the same time. If there is no direct access to the site, you'll need to arrange a suitable dropping point from which you can transport the materials by the barrow-load.

Excavating the site to any extent will leave you with a lot of spare soil. Unless you can dispose of this elsewhere in the garden, hire a *mini-skip* (you'll find them listed in Yellow Pages) for the days you dig.

Depending on how much help is available, you should allow two weekends for the job – one for the excavating and levelling, the other for the actual laying. Try to keep your plans flexible though – the one thing you can't organize is the weather, and laying a patio is not a job to do when it's raining.

Below: Laying slabs on dabs of mortar.

SETTING OUT AND EXCAVATING

Mark out the area of your patio using string lines and pegs, allowing a little extra all round. Check the area allows you to fit in a whole number of paving slabs, depending on your laying pattern.

The finished patio *must* slope away from the house to allow rainwater to drain safely away. The easiest way to create this slope, and at the same time ensure you dig down to a consistent depth, is to use a series of boards as shown to divide the site into bays of manageable width – about 1.5m (5') maximum.

Fitting levelling boards

1 Draw a chalk line along the house wall to indicate the finished height of the patio (at least 150mm (6") below the DPC).

2 Dig a trench about 150mm (6") deep along the wall, then wedge your first levelling boards in place so that their top edges are 50mm (2") below the chalk line.

3 Excavate the earth across the site roughly level with the base of the boards. Chock up a second row of boards parallel to the first, about 1.5m (5') away.

4 Use a spirit level and timber (see Tip) to set the height of the second row of boards. The block fixed to the timber ensures they will be an even 25mm (1") lower.

5 Repeat the procedure to fix the next row of boards 25mm (1") lower still. Afterwards, lay your wood across the rows of boards and check the site is roughly level.

On existing paving...

Follow the same procedure, but omitting the trench. Since you only need to gauge the depth of the sand, use 50mm (2") wide battens as levelling boards; wedge them in place on the paving with small stones.

If you have to dig up any turf when excavating, save it for finishing the edges (see overleaf).

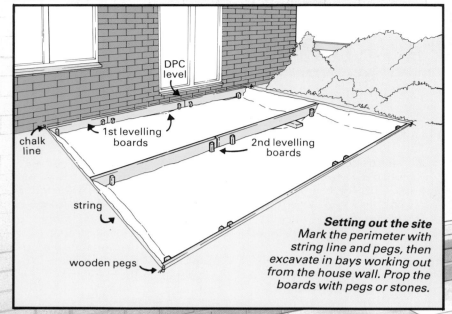

DPC level
1st levelling boards
2nd levelling boards
chalk line
string
wooden pegs

Setting out the site
Mark the perimeter with string line and pegs, then excavate in bays working out from the house wall. Prop the boards with pegs or stones.

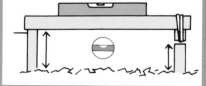

Trade tip

Gauging the slope

❛ Gauge the slope between bays by fitting a 25mm (1") thick piece of wood to the **lower** end of the timber on which you rest your spirit level. That way, when you get a level reading, you know the lower boards are in fact 25mm below the upper ones. ❜

LAYING THE HARDCORE

1 *Tip the hardcore into each bay, making sure it is packed well into the corners, but taking care not to dislodge any of the levelling boards.*

2 *Tamp the hardcore down with the end of a heavy piece of timber. If there are any high spots or large pieces of rubble, break them up with a hammer.*

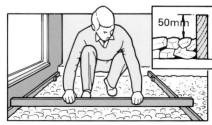

3 *Use a batten across the tops of the levelling boards to check that the level of the hardcore is about 50mm (2") below them right across the site.*

50mm

SPREADING THE SAND

1 Tip sand on top of the hardcore and rake it out roughly level with the tops of the levelling boards. Be sure that it fills any gaps.

2 Work across the first bay with your length of 100 × 50mm (4 × 2″) timber, tamping the sand down level with the tops of the levelling boards.

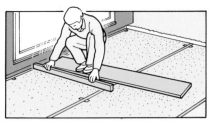

3 Continue in manageable stages until you have levelled the whole site. Kneel on a plank if you have to work over any area that's already been levelled.

50mm sand bed

50mm hardcore base

PLACING THE FIRST SLAB

Start laying the slabs against the house wall so that you have a square edge to work from – choose whichever side involves disturbing the sand the least.

If you are laying the slabs on mortar, mix this up near the site on a piece of old board. Add just enough water to bind the dry ingredients together and test by pressing your trowel into the mixture – the mark should remain visible.

1 Standing on a plank when you have to walk on the sand, ease out the levelling boards against the house wall and fill the gap with more sand.

2 Start laying against the house wall. If you are laying with mortar, drop five fist-sized dabs so that they fall within the area of your slab as shown.

3 Lay the first slab square to the house wall. Take care not to drop one corner first so it digs into the sand. Tap it with the shaft of the hammer to level.

COMPLETING THE PAVING

Build up the paving as shown, referring to your laying plan. Slide rather than lift the slabs into place, and wherever possible spread the weight so you don't disturb those already laid.

Check the alignment as you go, while there's still room for manoeuvre; if necessary, slip thin pieces of wood between the slabs to keep the spacing even.

Complete the whole slabs before filling in with any cut ones. When cutting the slabs, make sure you wear proper eye protection.

1 *Resting the edge of a second slab on the first, draw it across so that it drops cleanly into place. Repeat this to complete the first row.*

2 *Start to add the second row of slabs, using the ones which you have already laid to take the weight of the slab you are about to position.*

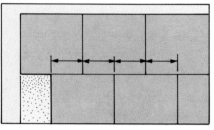

3 *Check the alignment of the slabs - particularly if you are building up a staggered pattern. It is easy to correct at this stage – but not later.*

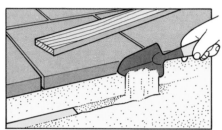

4 *Carry on building up the paving row by row until the site is covered. When you come to a levelling board, ease it out and fill the gap with sand.*

5 *At the edges, backfill with earth to stop the sand bed 'creeping'. If you removed any turf, cut this to size and lay it in place against the slabs.*

CUTTING AND FINISHING

1 *Chalk cutting lines all round any slabs which need cutting. Use a club hammer and bolster to chip a groove along the marked line on both sides and the edges.*

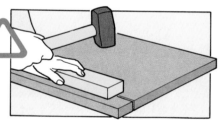

2 *Lay a block of wood over the cutting line and tap hard to split the slab. Make sure you wear goggles during both steps, to protect your eyes.*

3 *When all the slabs are laid, fill around the patio with earth or turf and brush sand across the entire surface to fill the cracks in the paving.*

PROBLEM SOLVER

Dealing with a gully

It's quite possible that there will be a drainage gully on the house wall to take rainwater running off the roof. This must not be disturbed, but should be incorporated into the patio.

The gully will have a grille set in concrete, which may have a bricked-in surround. When you excavate the site, work carefully in this area so as not to crack the gully or its surround.

If there's an existing surround, lay your slabs leaving a gap around this. When the patio is complete, cut pieces to fit in the gaps, filling in with sand to adjust the level.

If there isn't a surround, fit one to stop water splashing on the patio. Use a pre-cast concrete surround (from a builder's merchant), bedded in mortar on the old concrete.

Concrete surrounds (right, inset) come in various sizes. Bed one on top of the old gully surround on blobs of bricklaying mortar. When set, fill around the surround with a cut slab and more sand.

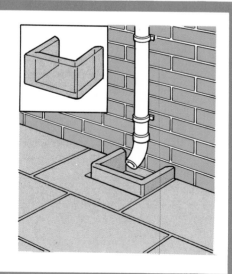

FITTING A PATIO AWNING

Not everyone wants to sunbathe on their patio – many people prefer to sit out in shade. What's more, strong sunlight can rapidly fade curtains, carpets and upholstery inside the house, so if you have patio doors or large expanses of window, it's actually a good idea to screen them from direct sun.

The best way to provide shade is to fit a patio awning or canopy which can be extended when needed and neatly retracted when the sun goes down. This also gives the bonus that summer showers won't threaten your enjoyment of a warm day.

Most modern awnings have a mechanism similar to a roller blind, with arms to extend them at an angle from the wall. The alternative is a *sectional awning* – commonly called a Dutch canopy.

An awning provides shade for your patio and helps to protect furnishings from direct sunlight.

....Shopping List....

Awnings are mainly sold by specialist suppliers (look under 'Blinds and Awnings' in Yellow Pages). Most will install as well, which is generally worth paying for on all but the smallest types.

There are three basic types of awning, all of which usually have a maintenance-free aluminium alloy frame covered with a range of fabrics, from plain waterproofed canvas to bright coloured plastic.

Drop arm awnings are the cheapest. Hinged arms fixed to the wall at each side fall towards the horizontal as the awning extends; some are non-adjustable, others can be slid up or down vertical tracks to vary the angle and projection of the awning. With some designs, the projecting arms may be an awkward obstacle to tall people.

Retractable arm awnings avoid this problem by having folding supports under the blind itself, above head height. The arms fold back on themselves so that when closed they are hidden by the front of the awning. This type tends to be more expensive than drop arm awnings, but can give a bigger shade area.

Dutch canopies have a distinctive shape like a pram hood and come with either a curved or a flat top. They are good for shading a window, but provide hardly any shade for sitting out of doors.

After deciding on the type of awning and choosing a fabric, you need to take detailed measurements. Most suppliers offer a small range of standard sizes, and also make to measure (usually at a slightly higher price). In fact, it rarely matters much if the awning or canopy is slightly wider or narrower than the ideal, so long as it is in proportion to the window. Normally, awnings are slightly wider than the windows they are shading, while Dutch canopies should clear the opening by about 200mm (8″) all round.

Fixings Lightweight blinds can sometimes be fixed with screws and wallplugs, but for heavier awnings use masonry anchors.

Tools checklist: Access equipment, tape measure, spirit level, drill and masonry bits (a large bit is needed for masonry anchors), spanners, screwdrivers.

drop arm awning

retractable arm awning

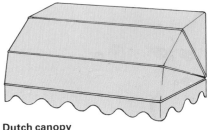

Dutch canopy

CHOOSING AN AWNING

DROP ARM AWNINGS

Drop arm awnings (also called 'window awnings') normally extend to between 1.4 and 2.2m (4'6" to 7'3"). Maximum widths vary – some go up to around 3.5m (11'6"), while others may be twice this. (Separate blinds can also be linked together.).

The roller mechanism takes up very little space – typically around 150mm (6") square in cross section. Covers vary from a simple hood to a completely enclosed case with a solid front attached to the arms.

Most arms have fixed brackets, but some have sliding mounts, allowing you to raise the awning to walk underneath the sides.

Accessories may include security locking arms or spring mechanisms which help to steady the awning in a strong wind.

The arms may have fixed or sliding mounts and the front may form an enclosed case.

DUTCH CANOPIES

A Dutch canopy has a number of frame members which are hinged together at a common point, rather like the pages of a book. These are pulled up together against the wall when the canopy is retracted. As the frames open out they carry the fabric with them, and the lowest frame drops to the horizontal to form the familiar rounded shape.

The frames are available in a range of shapes from a rectangle to a semi-circle – the more curved the frame, the more space needed for fitting it above a window or door. Widths usually go up to around 3.5m (11'6"), but wider units can be made to order. Maximum projection is generally less than 1.5m (5').

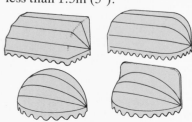

Curved frames come in a range of profiles for different decorative effects. However, fitting space may restrict your choice.

RETRACTABLE ARM AWNINGS

This type of awning can extend much further than other types, almost providing a temporary roof. The maximum projection depends on the design but can be as much as 3m (10′). The span is also much wider than other types – up to 16m (52′6″) or so.

Unlike most drop arm awnings, the blind angle is adjustable – it can extend horizontally or point downwards as much as you want. The mechanism is totally contained within the roller frame, which is typically no more than 200mm (8″) high and 150mm (6″) deep.

A hood to protect the furled blind is normally included as part of the kit. With some designs a solid front rail fits flush against this to form an enclosed box.

Retractable arm awnings can be adjusted to project at any angle to the wall – even horizontally.

Trade tip

Under the eaves

❝ Where the awning or canopy is to be fixed hard up against overhanging eaves, it can either be mounted using a special soffit (top-fixing) bracket, or suspended from the overhanging rafter ends where no soffit board has been fitted. Some manufacturers offer multi-purpose brackets which can be face-fixed or top-hung, according to the mounting position.

AUTOMATIC OPERATION

Most extending awnings are fitted with a removable winding handle, but some expensive models have optional electric operation via a 'tubular motor' concealed within the roller itself. A simple two-position switch controls the awning operation, and there are built-in stops to prevent over-extension. Motorised operation is particularly valuable if you fit an awning to an inaccessible upper storey window.

Dutch canopies are generally raised and lowered with a cord and pulley arrangement; the cord is released to allow the blind to drop into its fully extended position, and is drawn up and tied off around a wall-mounted cleat to raise it. With upstairs windows, special pulleys are fitted so the pull cords pass through the window frame and can be operated from inside the room. Again, motorised operation is available.

Motorised awnings can even be linked to sensors within the room providing automatic control as temperatures change.

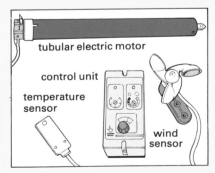

Tubular electric motors roll the blind in and out. They can be hand-switched or linked to temperature and wind sensors for automatic operation.

INSTALLING AN AWNING

Small awnings can be fitted fairly easily. Large ones are awkward to handle, so you need good access equipment and an assistant. In such cases it is usually simpler and just as cheap to have them installed by the supplier.

Most types come virtually fully assembled. All you normally have to do is ensure the awning is set level and fixed firmly – a strong fixing is obviously all-important as the wind can exert a considerable force on an extended blind. Assembly details vary slightly from model to model, so follow the manufacturer's instructions where appropriate.

Roller-type awnings of all types are supplied furled on the roller. This normally simply fits on brackets which are attached to the wall with appropriate heavy-duty fixings. With drop-arm awnings, the drop arms must then be screwed in place, while retractable arms may have to be fitted separately after extending the blind.

Dutch canopies are supplied ready-assembled, complete with fabric cover. The rear frame member is fixed to the wall by hooking it on to U-shaped brackets and then screwing the bottoms of the frames in place – small canopies usually have two brackets, wider ones three or even four. All you have to do is mount the brackets on the wall, then fit the pull-cord mechanism.

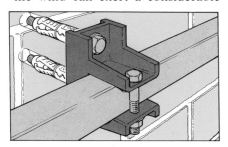

1 **With roller-type awnings**, secure the fixing brackets in place using masonry anchors. Then offer up the roller and lock it into place on the brackets.

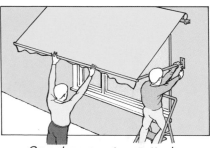

2 On a drop-arm type, attach the arms to the front rail. With a helper, mark the positions of the mounting plates at each side, then screw them to the wall.

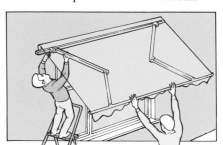

3 Retractable arm types may be fully assembled. On some types, you need a helper to extend the awning while you fit the spring-loaded arms in place.

1 **With a Dutch canopy**, screw the U-shaped hanging brackets to the wall making sure they are level and that they won't foul the pulleys.

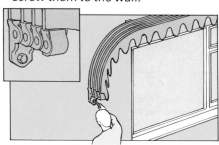

2 Hook the rear frame over the brackets, then screw the bottom ends of the frame to the wall to fix the canopy firmly in position.

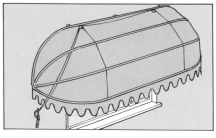

3 Thread the pull-cord and test the operation of the canopy. Fit a wall cleat and tie off the cord, or run it indoors on pulleys mounted on the window.

PROBLEM SOLVER

Fixing to problem surfaces

Whatever fixing method is being used, it is important that the wall is clear of obstructions such as flues, downpipes and overflows. It is also essential to fix into sound material. Take extra care with walls made from lightweight aggregate blocks, and don't use expanding wall anchors close to the edge of masonry or you may find that they split the bricks.

Sound but uneven surfaces (for example, heavily textured rendering or pebbledash) may need chipping away to provide a smooth base. Alternatively, use wooden packing blocks behind the mountings so that they sit squarely against the wall.

Tile-hung or cladding finishes must be removed to allow the blind mechanism to be installed – either directly to the masonry beneath, or to a substantial timber wall-plate screwed and anchored to the wall.

It is usually possible to cut out small areas of timber or plastic cladding without disturbing the rest. A jigsaw is likely to be the best tool.

Tile hanging is often more complicated. The tiles will be nailed to battens, with each row covered by the one above, so you may have to strip them working from the top downwards to the level of the blind.

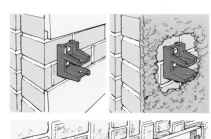

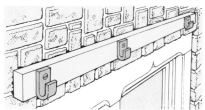

Pack out uneven surfaces to provide a level fixing. Cladding should be stripped so you can fix to firm masonry.

PAVING A PATH WITH BLOCKS

A path laid with patio pavers or blocks over a sand bed makes an attractive, as well as practical, addition to any garden. The technique is in fact very similar to laying a patio; the main difference is that the edges of the path must be finished with mortared-in edging blocks to stop the paving spreading.

Working out a design

Paving for paths comes in all shapes and sizes, but for practical purposes divides between patio-sized slabs as large as 600×450×38mm (24×18×1½"), and smaller blocks or bricks measuring around 200×100×50mm (8×4×2"). A variety of materials are used, concrete and reconstituted stone being the most common.

Slabs cover a larger area per unit, but their weight can make them unwieldy to lay. Blocks and bricks are easier to handle and offer a range of interesting laying patterns (see page 44). Their proportions may suit a small garden better, and they are easier to fit around awkward shapes – important if the path is to have bends in it.

Paving slabs and blocks are widely available from DIY superstores, builder's merchants and garden centres, all of whom should be able to supply your other requirements as well. Normally, it's best to check what's available, note the coverage per square metre or square foot of your chosen design, then draw up a scale plan of the path (see overleaf) and work out quantities from this.

Sand for bedding the paving should be laid to a depth of around 50mm (2"), but you'll need roughly 20% extra to cover wastage and filling the joints. Use *sharp sand*; insist to the supplier that it is delivered reasonably dry, or it will be difficult to bed in.

Hardcore may be needed to provide a firm base on loose or poorly drained subsoil – check by digging a test hole. You can either make your own from broken up brick and concrete, or arrange for a load to be delivered with the other materials. A depth of 50–100mm (2–4") should be sufficient.

Edging blocks (see overleaf) are available in cast concrete or reconstituted stone with rounded or square top edges. They are normally 900mm (3') long by 50mm (2") thick with a choice of 150mm, 200mm or 250mm (6", 8" or 10") depths.

Mortar for bedding the edging blocks is best bought in dry mixed form by the 25kg (55lb), 40kg (88lb) or 50kg (110lb) bag. You need roughly 15kg (33lb) per metre (yard) of path.

Very few special tools are needed apart from a levelling board, which you can make yourself from offcuts of timber (see overleaf). However, it may be worth hiring an *hydraulic brick splitter* if you have a lot of cutting to do. It's also worth hiring a *power compactor* if you're laying blocks or bricks.

Tools checklist: Spade, shovel, bucket, barrow, spirit level, string and pegs, club hammer, bolster (or brick splitter), tape measure, mixing board.

Small paving blocks usually measure 200×100×50mm (8×4×2") although thicknesses can vary.

Some types have a textured, non-slip surface; others are halved or quartered which makes them easier to cut. Specially shaped pavers are available for creating intricate patterns and designs.

Paving slabs are available in a range of sizes and can be as large as 600×450×38mm (24×18×1½").

Multi-block pavers (above) usually measure 450×450×40mm (18×18×1½").

Each slab is divided into sections which make up an attractive pattern when laid. Many types have a textured non-slip surface.

PREPARING THE SITE

Draw a scale plan of the proposed path (see right) and take this with you when ordering materials. Unlike a patio, you should be able to avoid obstructions such as drains and trees. Levels aren't critical either, although the path should slope slightly away from the house to allow for water run-off; if it butts up to the house, it must also finish at least 150mm (6") below the level of the damp-proof course.

Aim to make the width of the path a whole number of your chosen pavers to avoid unnecessary cutting – test-lay a few to check the measurement. If you're laying small pavers to a pattern (see page 44), draw a detailed sketch of the pattern to work out the path width.

Gauge the edging block depth by the thickness of the pavers and the depth of the bed plus 50mm. For example, for 50mm thick pavers and a 50mm thick sand bed, choose $50mm + 50mm + 50mm = 150mm$ deep blocks. If you have to lay hardcore, adjust the block depth accordingly.

The job divides neatly into stages:
■ Excavate trenches for the edging blocks and bed in place in mortar.
■ Excavate the ground between, then lay and level the sand bed.
■ Lay and level the pavers, fill in any spaces with cut pavers, then brush in sand to fill the joints.

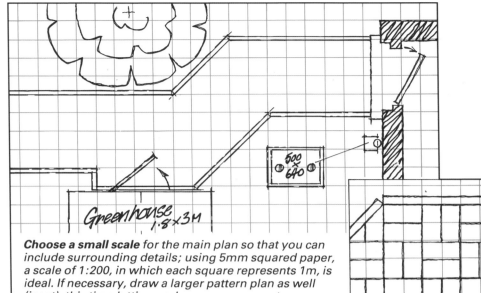

Greenhouse 1.8×3M

Choose a small scale for the main plan so that you can include surrounding details; using 5mm squared paper, a scale of 1:200, in which each square represents 1m, is ideal. If necessary, draw a larger pattern plan as well (inset), this time letting each square represent a square unit of your chosen paver size.

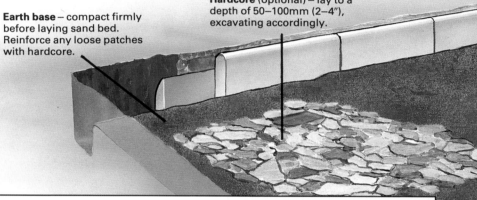

Earth base – compact firmly before laying sand bed. Reinforce any loose patches with hardcore.

Hardcore (optional) – lay to a depth of 50–100mm (2–4"), excavating accordingly.

EXCAVATING AND EDGING

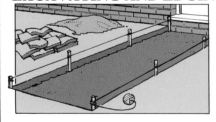

1 Mark the final edges of the path with lengths of string stretched taut between wooden pegs. Remove any vegetation and topsoil between the lines.

2 Dig trenches for the edging blocks using the lines as a guide. They should be about 100mm (4") wide, and around 50mm (2") deeper than the blocks.

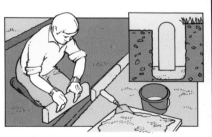

3 Starting at one end, mix up a batch of mortar and shovel it into the trenches. Then start bedding the edging blocks so that they're flush with ground level.

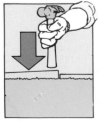

4 Check periodically that the blocks sit level. Tap with a hammer handle to lower, or lift and pack in more mortar underneath.

5 Then check that the rows sit level with each other by placing a spirit level and timber straightedge between them. Check that the spacing is constant too.

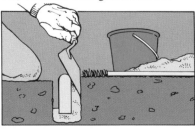

6 Trowel in more mortar along the outside edges of the blocks to hold them in place. Smooth to a curved profile, cover with soil, and leave to harden.

MAKING A LEVELLING BOARD

Knock up a home-made levelling board to help excavate the rest of the soil and lay the sand bed.

■ Cut a straight length of batten a little longer than the span across the edgings.

■ Cut a plank about 100–150mm (4–6") wide to the exact width of the path.

■ Nail or screw both pieces together so that the plank projects from the batten by about 6mm (¼") more than the thickness of your paving.

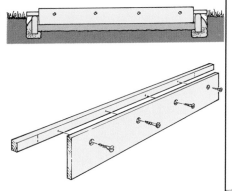

Sand bed – level using home-made levelling board.

If path adjoins house, it must be at least 150mm (6") below the DPC.

Bed pavers directly in sand. Brush in more sand to fill the joints.

Bed edging blocks in mortar. Pack outer edges with more mortar, then cover with soil.

Trade tip

Weeding out

❝ I always spray a long-lasting weedkiller (such as sodium chlorate) over excavations, especially shallow ones like those needed for a path. This kills off any lingering roots that might sprout up through the blocks later. ❞

SPREADING THE SAND BED

1 Dig out the soil between the edging blocks to allow for the thickness of the pavers and 50mm (2") sand bed. Use the levelling board as a rough depth guide.

2 After levelling up, compact the soil firmly with a heavy timber baulk. (If the ground is unstable, dig deeper, then lay and compact a layer of hardcore.)

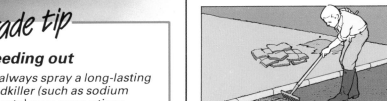

3 Shovel the sand over the compacted soil base. Use a rake to spread it to roughly the right depth all over, then damp down with a watering can.

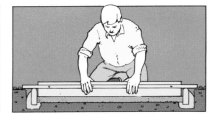

4 Rest your levelling board on the edging blocks and scrape back and forth to smooth out the sand. Work backwards from one end, then remove any surplus.

LAYING THE PAVERS

Laying the pavers is straightforward enough, but take care to position them correctly first time, otherwise the sand bed will soon get uneven. Where appropriate, sketch out the laying pattern (see below) on paper and keep this with you as a guide.

Take care not to step on the sand. Where you can't work from the edges, lay a board down over the bedded pavers to crouch on.

Whether or not you have to use a compactor depends on how successful you are at levelling the pavers; with luck, you shouldn't need to.

1 Start positioning the pavers at one end of the path. Don't force them into the sand – **lay them on top**. Butt adjacent pavers tightly against each other.

2 Crouching on a board, lay the pavers in strict sequence so you don't confuse the pattern. Leave any cut pavers until the end (see Problem Solver).

LAYING PATTERNS

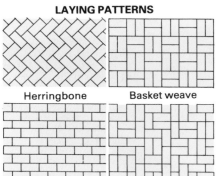

Herringbone   Basket weave

Staggered   Random

3 Use a block of wood and club hammer to level the pavers. If one sinks, lever it up and add more bedding sand until it lies flush with its neighbours.

4 You may need to use a power compactor with a rubber sole plate for final levelling. Afterwards, brush more sand over the path to fill the joints.

PROBLEM SOLVER

Filling in spaces

Cutting pavers to fit awkward spaces is generally the trickiest part of the job.

If the paving material is reasonably soft and there isn't much cutting to do, you can get by using a bolster and club hammer. Do the cutting on a bed of sand and be sure to wear some form of eye protection.

A more reliable method – essential for hard materials such as engineering bricks – is to hire a brick splitter like the one shown on the right. This cuts thinner and more cleanly than a bolster, and is good for 'nibbling' away small corners for an accurate fit.

Cutting with a bolster: chip a thin cutting line right around the paver. Then lay it on sand, place the bolster on the cutting line, and strike smartly.

Using a brick splitter: mark a cutting line across the paver in chalk or pencil, then position the paver in the jaws of the machine, and crank the handle to split. Turn your eyes away as you do so, to guard against flying chips of masonry.

BUILDING A SCREEN BLOCK WALL

Decorative screen block walls combine lightness with a fair degree of privacy – two qualities which generally make them first choice for garden building jobs such as screening a patio or defining a boundary close to the house.

From a do-it-yourselfer's point of view, screen blocks also have the distinct advantage of being easy to lay. And if you've never done any building before, constructing a screen block wall is the perfect introduction to the more demanding skill of bricklaying.

What are screen blocks?

Screen blocks are made of high quality dense concrete and are mostly off-white, though you may find other colours available. The majority are *pierced*, both to save weight and to create the characteristic decorative effect. A range of different pierced patterns is available, some of which are based on single blocks, and others on modules of four blocks. You can also buy solid screen blocks which have a pattern pressed deeply into their faces, though the choice is rather limited.

Screen blocks are unsuitable for loadbearing walls, and because they are always laid unbonded – that is,

Screen wall blocks, pillars and cappings come in easy-to-handle modular sizes, making them easy to lay.

they do not overlap – they have only limited sideways strength. For this reason any wall of significant size needs reinforcing at intervals with pillars built using compatible *pilaster* blocks.

In spite of these limitations, screen blocks have many uses besides decorative walls:

■ As supports for a lightweight lean-to roof over a carport or covered way.
■ As garden planters.
■ As screening for a dustbin area or coal store.
■ As 'top-ups' for a low garden wall to provide extra privacy, shade, or interesting light patterns.

A screen wall *is perfect for gaining extra privacy (left) without totally excluding light. Blocks can also be used to enclose outdoor areas like the pergola above, in which case they can go on top of the foundations or on a low wall.*

DESIGNING A BLOCK WALL

A screen block wall can be built on existing concrete paving, or on paving slabs bedded in mortar (slabs laid in sand are unsuitable). The site must be level, though any slight unevenness can be taken up by the mortar used to bed the first row of blocks in place.

On grass or bare earth, cast a concrete strip foundation specially for the purpose; it should measure 100mm (4″) thick by 300mm (12″) wide and should extend 100mm (4″) beyond the wall at the ends and at corners.

Although screen blocks are sold in both metric and Imperial sizes, for practical purposes you can reckon on them measuring 300×300×100mm (12×12×4″) including an allowance for 10mm (⅜″) mortar joints. The maximum recommended height for a block wall is 1.8m (6′); above this, the blocks become difficult to handle and extra reinforcement is needed.

For walls up to 600mm (2′) high, it's a good idea to reinforce the pillars with metal bars; above this height it is essential. Ideally the bars should be bedded into the foundations, or mortared into holes cut into an existing base.

Pilaster blocks typically measure 190×194×194mm (about 7½×7½×7⅝″) and come in three types; *end, intermediate,* and *corner.* Allow three pilaster blocks per two rows of screen blocks.

Position pillars at the ends, at corners, and every 3m (10′) along the wall.

Coping blocks for finishing the top of the wall generally measure 610× 140mm (24× 5½″) and come in 25mm (1″) thicknesses. and 50mm (2″) tops

Capping block

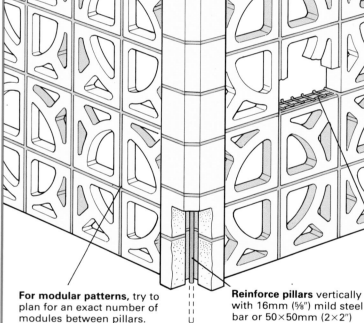

Trade tip

Against a house wall...

❝ If you're building up against house wall, strengthen the construction with metal **wall ties** at 600mm (2′) intervals. Bed these into the mortar beds of the pilaster blocks or capping, and into slots cut in the brickwork.

It's also advisable to bed a strip of 100mm (4″) damp-proofing felt into the mortar between the pillar and house wall, to protect the brickwork from penetrating damp. ❞

For modular patterns, try to plan for an exact number of modules between pillars.

Reinforce pillars vertically with 16mm (⅝″) mild steel bar or 50×50mm (2×2″) angle iron bedded into the foundations.

For high walls (over 600mm/2′), bed galvanized *tramline reinforcing strips* into the joints between blocks.

....Shopping List....

You'll find it helpful to draw a scale plan of the proposed wall, both to work out the number of blocks needed, and as a reminder of what else to buy. Draw the plan on 5mm squared paper, to a scale of 1:60 – one square per block.
Screen blocks are sold by garden centres, superstores and builders' merchants. They weigh about 9kg (20lb) each, so have them delivered if possible.
Concrete for the foundations should be the standard general-purpose mix – 1 part cement, 2½ parts sharp sand and 3½ parts aggregate, or 1 part cement to 5 parts all-in ballast.

Mortar for bedding the blocks should be standard mix of 1 part cement to 3 parts soft sand. However, many suppliers sell dry-mixed mortar specially formulated for screen block laying. One bucketful of dry mixed material will lay about 15 blocks.
Reinforcing bars, wall ties and mesh may only be obtainable from a builders' merchant. Bar length should cover at least two thirds of the pillar.
Tools checklist: Bricklaying trowel, spirit level, bolster, club hammer, shovel, buckets, spotboard, pegs and string, tape measure, wood dowel or piece of garden hose.

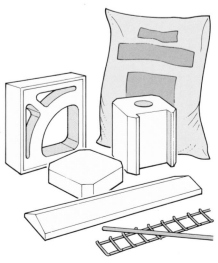

SETTING OUT

If you are using reinforcement for the pillars, set out the first row of blocks in a dry run to fix the pillar positions. The cavities inside the pillar blocks allow some room for manoeuvre, but it's a good idea to set the bars as accurately as you can.

On existing foundations, chop out holes for the bars with a hammer and bolster (wear goggles to protect your eyes), then bed the bars in a strong mix of 1:3 mortar.

On new foundations, do the setting out just as the concrete begins to harden, then drive the bars into it and prop vertically.

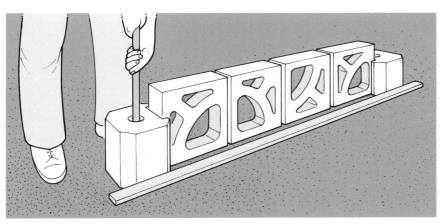

Set out a row of blocks in a dry run – allowing 10mm (⅜") for the mortar joints – to fix the positions of the pillars, then mark the reinforcing bar positions.

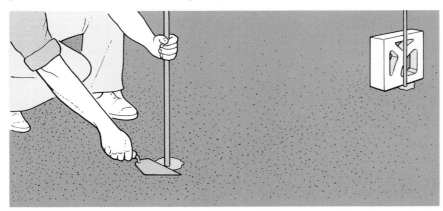

Chop out 100mm (4") deep holes for the bars, bed them in mortar, and prop temporarily. (If you are laying foundations, bed the bars in the concrete as it sets.)

PROBLEM SOLVER

Getting even joints

If you've never laid bricks or blocks before, you'll find the most difficult part is getting the mortar joints to an even 10mm (⅜") width so that everything lines up. The secret is in the way you handle the trowel, and since there's no substitute for experience it's worth practising with a test batch of mortar before you start block laying.

Run through the sequence shown and test with a block until you find the size of 'sausage' which produces a 10mm joint width with a minimum of adjustment.

Cut the mortar into sausage shapes on the spotboard . . .

. . . **pick up** a 'sausage' on the inside of the trowel . . .

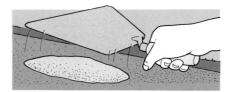

. . . **deposit it** on the base with a flick of the wrist . . .

. . . **then indent it** to provide for adjustment when bedding down.

BUILDING UP THE WALL

1 Lay a bed of mortar for the first pilaster block, set in position and check for level. Adjust as required, then fill in the cavity with more mortar.

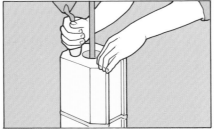

2 Lay a bed of mortar on the first pilaster block and bed a second block on top, checking that the joint is an even 10mm (⅜"). Then lay a third block.

3 Trowel a bed of mortar along the line of the wall, then spread more on the edge of the first block. Set in place against the pillar and check the level.

4 Lay a bed of mortar on the first screen block, then repeat the sequence for a second screen block. Check it sits level with the pilaster blocks.

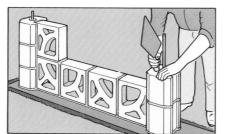

5 Lay the rest of the first row of screen blocks, then build up on the second pillar in the same way as the first. Keep a constant check on the levels.

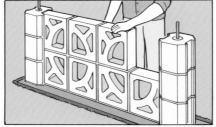

6 Fill in the remaining screen blocks. You can now repeat steps 1–6 for each two rows of screen blocks, or for another complete section of wall.

If you like, you can use a string line stretched taut between the ends of the wall as a guide to laying intervening blocks – but always check each one for level.

FINISHING OFF

Lay the copings and cappings which finish the top of the wall, bedding them on mortar in the same way as the blocks.

If you need to cut a coping block to fit, measure it against the space and score a cutting line right around it – not forgetting to allow for the space taken up by the mortar joint.

Then lay the block on a bed of sand and convert the cutting line into a thin groove using a hammer and bolster. One sharp tap with the bolster should then be enough to make it split along the marked line.

The final stage is to brush off any surplus mortar and rub down the mortar joints until they have a smooth and even finish.

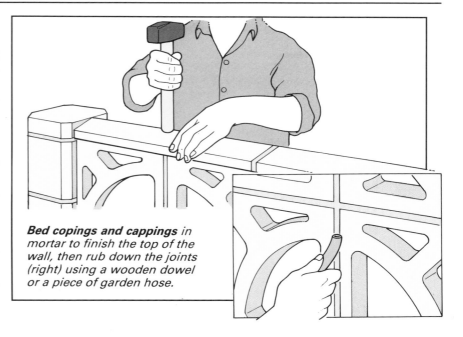

Bed copings and cappings in mortar to finish the top of the wall, then rub down the joints (right) using a wooden dowel or a piece of garden hose.

REPAIRING FENCES AND WOODEN GATES

Fences take a considerable battering every time there's a strong wind. And because the exposed timber frequently gets wet, it is more than usually prone to rot. Prevention is much better than cure, so carry out an annual inspection (see below) and repair any damage quickly.

There are three basic types of wooden fence:

Panel fences have prefabricated panels made of thin slats nailed to a framework and fitted between wooden or slotted concrete posts. The slats can be arranged in different patterns, but are always quite thin and in time are likely to split. Most panels are given a long-term preservative treatment but they can rot relatively quickly once this wears off – unless re-treated. Posts can also suffer from rot, especially close to the ground.

Close-boarded fences have feather-edge boards nailed to arris rails fixed between wooden or concrete posts. Rot is most likely to affect the bases of the posts or the points where the rails join the posts. The boards can split if they are fixed too firmly, without allowing for expansion and contraction, and their bases may rot if in contact with the ground.

Palisades (palings) have an open construction with large gaps left between the boards. Rot tends to affect the same areas as on close-boarded fence. Palisades are often painted – and paint breaks down more quickly than preservative, allowing damp to penetrate and collect but not dry out again.

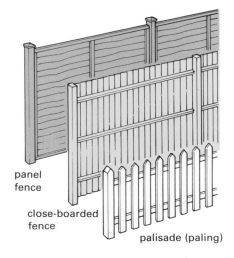

panel fence

close-boarded fence

palisade (paling)

The main types of fence. Each has particular weak points resulting from the way it is built.

PREVENTIVE MAINTENANCE

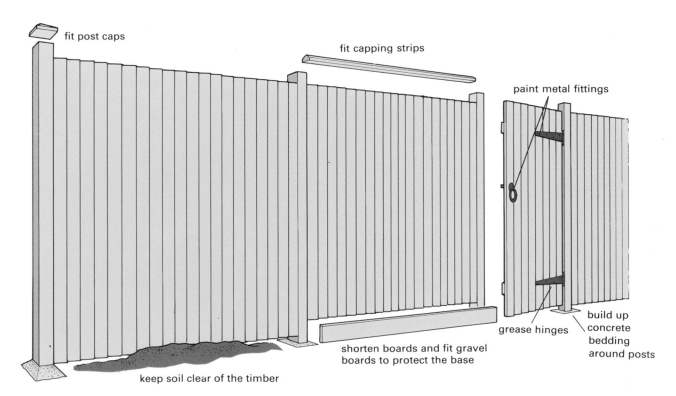

fit post caps

fit capping strips

paint metal fittings

grease hinges

build up concrete bedding around posts

shorten boards and fit gravel boards to protect the base

keep soil clear of the timber

■ Treat bare timber regularly to ward off rot – re-apply a creosote finish every 2–3 years to maintain the quality of finish.

■ Repaint gates, palings, etc when the old paint shows signs of breaking down.

■ Paint latches, hinges and other metal fittings with rust-resisting primer/paint. Renew when the paint film starts to break down.

■ Grease hinges frequently to prevent binding.

■ Prevent soil from piling up around the bases of boards, and fit a gravel board if none is present.

■ Keep soil away from the bases of posts. Build up a concrete cap if necessary in order to shoot water away from the wood.

■ Fit caps to the posts or fencing panels to prevent water from soaking into the exposed end grain and causing rot.

REPAIRING A BROKEN POST

Posts normally give way where they enter the ground, due to rot damage. The simple cure is a metal or concrete repair spur.

Metal spurs have a socket into which the base of the post is driven. They are easy to use when the post has been bedded in concrete, but aren't suitable when the affected post carries a gate; the weight is likely to prove too much. They are also only normally available for 75mm (3″) posts. When the post is loose in an otherwise sound concrete base, another option is to pull it out and set another post into the same socket (see Tip).

Concrete spurs are coachbolted to the old post and give a durable fixing that can be used with any size of post. However, they can't easily be used where there is existing concrete around the post, unless you excavate to remove it.

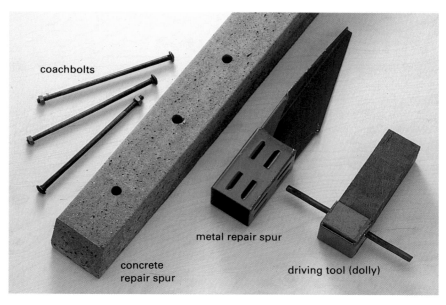

coachbolts

metal repair spur

concrete repair spur

driving tool (dolly)

Metal or concrete repair spurs can be used to deal with most problems where a post has rotted or broken at the base but is otherwise sound.

1 *To fit a metal repair spur,* support the fence and saw the old post flush with the concrete bedding. It may be reusable; otherwise, fit a new post.

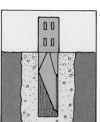

2 Prop the fence out of the way and drive in the spur following the old post's position. Use the special driving tool (dolly) and a sledge hammer.

3 Set the post in the spur's socket and hammer it home; metal barbs grip it firmly. Refix the fencing panels to the post as necessary.

1 *To fit a concrete spur,* prop the fence and cut the post back until you reach sound wood. It doesn't matter how far up you have to go.

2 Dig a hole at least 300mm (12″) square next to the post position. Make it about 500–600mm (20–24″) deep and fill the base with hardcore.

Trade tip

Use the old socket

❛Where a post has rotted in a sound concrete socket, just drop in a new one.

Prop the fence and free the post from its adjacent panels or arris rails. Pull it out using a lever made from sturdy timber over a block or pile of bricks. Lash the end of the lever to the post, tying off around a nail.

If this doesn't work, try fitting a stout bolt through the post and using a car jack to force it upwards.❜

3 Fit the spur up against the post and knock the bolts hard through the holes to mark their positions. Then remove the spur and drill through the post.

4 Refit the spur and bolt it to the post. Ram hardcore around it, followed by general purpose concrete mix. Tamp down and prop for 24 hours.

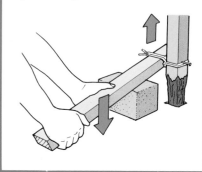

RENEWING BOARDS

Panel fences use standard sized panels which are easily replaced in one go. The only exception is at the ends, where panels may have been cut down to fit a smaller gap.

Close-boarded fences use individual boards which can be replaced separately if a single one has split. You may have to prise a couple of boards loose in order to free the one trapped between them.

■ If rusty nails have caused the boards to come loose, renail with 50mm (2″) galvanized nails.

■ If all the boards are rotting at the base, saw them short and fit a new gravel board to make up the difference.

Gravel boards are there to protect the base of the fence – so if they rot it is only because they are doing their job. A gravel board can normally simply be knocked free from its fixings. If it is slotted into grooves in the posts, first saw through to free it, then replace with a new board cut to fit. Fit the board in the old groove at one end, and nail the other to a short peg knocked into the ground.

1 *Remove a broken panel by pulling out the fixings. You may have to slide the panel upwards or remove some brackets to free it easily.*

2 *Slot a new panel into the fixings. If tight, ease the edge with a plane; if loose, pack out with a slip of wood. Nonstandard panels must be cut down.*

Nail on new featheredge boards after prising loose adjacent boards to free the damaged ones. Fix with galvanized nails and renail the other loose boards.

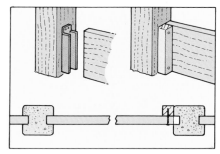

Replace a gravel board with the clips or battens used to fix the old one. Where previously slotted, fit one end this way and fit the second to a peg.

REPAIRING A BROKEN ARRIS RAIL

Galvanized steel arris rail brackets are sold by suppliers of fencing materials; there are two types. *Straight* brackets are for repairing a split in the middle of a rail or splicing in a new section. *Flanged* post brackets can be used to rejoin a rail to a post.

Fix with galvanized steel screws (eg chipboard screws) or galvanized fencing nails. Screws have an advantage in that you don't need to hammer a weakened fence.

When an arris rail is seriously damaged (for example, bowed in the centre), it is often better to replace it entirely.

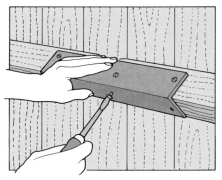

Screw on a straight bracket to support an arris rail which has split in the middle. Prop the fence if you need to pull the rail straight.

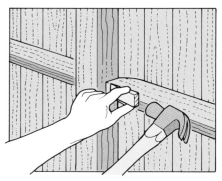

Lock a loose joint in place by hammering a glued wedge into the mortise and tenon joint. This gives a firmer fixing than trying to nail it.

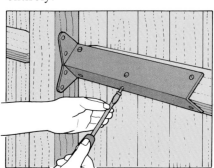

Strengthen a very weak joint by screwing on a flanged post bracket. Remove any rot and treat the wood with preservative first to prevent problems later.

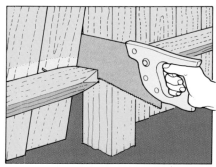

Remove an arris rail by hammering from the back to spring the nails free. Pull them out and try to work the rail out. If it won't come, saw through the rail.

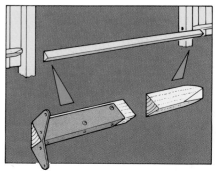

Fit a new rail by cutting a tenon at one end and inserting this first. Fasten the other end with a flanged bracket, then renail the boards.

REPAIRING GATES

When gates show signs of rot, repair the damage as soon as possible to prevent it affecting the strength of the frame. Superficial rot can be patched with resin wood filler or a rot care system; larger sections such as panelling are better replaced with new wood. Treat all the replacement timber with preservative.

If a gate has started to sag, this may be due to loose joints or loose hinges.

■ Strengthen weak joints with metal brackets or dismantle and reglue the mortise and tenons with waterproof woodworking adhesive. Insert dowels through the joints to strengthen them.

■ If hinges have worked loose, renew the fixings. If they have worn badly, replace with new ones and keep them well greased to prevent a recurrence.

Problem areas (right). Gates are commonly the first part of a fence to show signs of age — check these symptoms to help you decide on the best remedy.

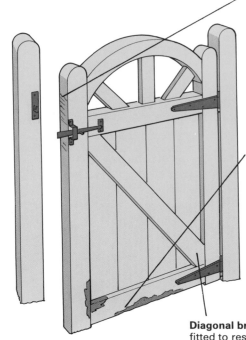

Binding at the top or underneath is often caused by the gate frame having dropped due to weak joints. It may also be due to the post leaning over or coming loose at the base.
■ Pull on the post to see whether it is firm.
■ Lift the gate to see whether the frame is loose or whether the hinges are worn/loose.

Rot usually affects the bottom first, especially in areas which trap water. Probe with a knife point to see how far it extends.
■ Superficial rot can be patched with a repair kit or new wood.
■ Badly rotted boarding can be replaced completely.
■ If frame joints are seriously affected, the gate probably needs replacement.

Diagonal bracing should be fitted to resist sagging. It must run in the direction shown to be effective.

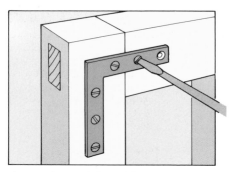

Strengthen a joint *with a metal repair bracket. Paint with a rust-resisting primer first as these brackets are almost always made from mild steel.*

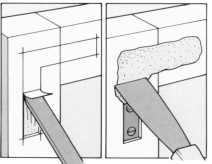

For a neater repair, *recess the bracket. Use a sharp knife to cut the outline and a chisel to remove the waste. After fitting, cover with resin wood filler.*

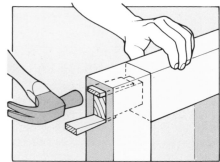

Where the whole frame is weak, *dismantle the joints and reglue the mortises and tenons. Cut new wedges and tap them in, to lock the joints.*

◼ PROBLEM SOLVER

Bracing a gate

Many gates have a simple rectangular frame which relies on the strength of its joints to prevent sagging. This type of construction can be made much stronger by adding a diagonal brace which locks the frame rigidly. The brace should run upwards from the hinge side if it is to be really effective.

Remove the gate and lay it on a firm surface. Pull it square and check the diagonals to ensure that they measure the same. Then cut a brace from timber of similar dimensions to the main frame and fix it firmly between the frame members.

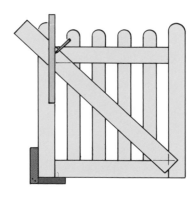

Pull the frame square, *then cut a piece of wood to fit the diagonal across the inside. Mark and saw this very carefully — it needs to be a perfect fit.*

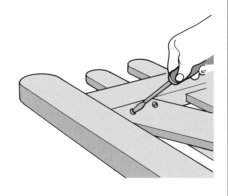

Treat the timber *before fixing the brace in place. Glue and screw it to the frame using waterproof woodworking adhesive and zinc-plated screws.*

PUTTING UP A PANEL FENCE

If you want a solid wooden fence, panel fencing is the logical choice. It's considerably cheaper than the close boarded type, and takes a fraction of the time to put up.

Although you can buy the panels, posts and other parts separately, complete kits are widely available from DIY superstores and garden centres. These tend to feature wooden (as opposed to concrete) posts, and include special fixings to make assembly easier. All the timber is pre-treated against rot.

The first step is to get to know what the various parts are, since there is a choice of fitting methods. After that, run through the design options overleaf and then work out your requirements in detail.

Panel fencing is a quick and relatively inexpensive way to gain extra privacy.

PARTS OF A PANEL FENCE

Fence panels are made to a standard width of 1.8m (6'). Common heights are 900mm, 1.2m, 1.5m and 1.8m (3', 4', 5' and 6'), though some designs are available in other sizes too.

Fixing clips for panels come in several patterns. The clips are nailed or screwed to the fence posts, then the panels are slotted into them and secured using more nails.

It's also possible to nail the panels direct to the posts using 50 or 75mm (2 or 3") galvanized nails (12 per panel), but in practice this involves more work.

Wooden posts are sold in a range of heights to match different sized panels, and in two thicknesses – 75mm (3") and 100mm (4") square. Unless you're joining the fence to an existing wall, buy one more than the number of panels you need.

Gravel boards fit at the base of the fence to stop the panels touching the ground and rotting. They can be nailed to the posts, or held in clip fixings (cleats).

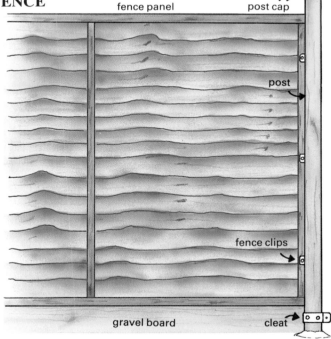

fence panel   post cap

post

fence clips

gravel board   cleat

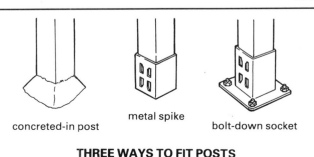

concreted-in post   metal spike   bolt-down socket

THREE WAYS TO FIT POSTS

Post caps are nailed on top of the posts to stop them rotting. Various styles are available, in wood or galvanized steel.

Post anchorages can be concrete (cheap, and better for unstable ground) or metal sockets (easy to use, and essential when fixing to an existing concrete path or patio).

For concreted-in posts allow an extra 450mm (18") on the post height if the fence is below 1.2m (4') high – and at least 600mm (2') for a higher fence.

Bed the posts in pre-dug holes using ready mixed coarse concrete mix. A 25kg (40lb) bag is enough for around 6 posts.

Metal post sockets are compatible with standard post sizes. Some types are adjustable, allowing for small errors in alignment.
■ On bare ground use spiked sockets. These can be driven in with a sledge hammer.
■ On concrete or stone, use bolt-down sockets. These take M10 expanding wall anchors (such as Rawlbolts).

DESIGNING A PANEL FENCE

Consider the following points when designing your new fence:

■ The ideal height for a boundary fence is 1.2m (4'). This gives privacy without obscuring the view.

■ Higher panels can create a 'closed in' feeling where space is limited – along the side of the house, for example. Where you need more privacy, think about fitting lower panels with garden trellis above them.

■ For maximum privacy, choose close boarded or waney edged panels. For sectioning off areas, open-weave interlocking or trellis panels are easier on the eye.

■ Around a patio, think about 'stepping' the panel sizes: fit high ones nearest the house for maximum privacy, and lower ones further away for a less restricted view.

See Problem Solver if you plan to build the fence on a sloping site.

You and your neighbours

It may seem obvious, but if the fence is to run along a boundary you should check before starting that it is your responsibility and not your neighbours. You can't just assume the posts are on the owner's side – the only reliable guide is the plan included with the house deeds.

At the same time, it is only fair to give your neighbour advance warning of your plans. Putting up the fence will inevitably affect their

garden, though you can reduce the disturbance by laying walking boards over flower beds or grass.

Finally, don't forget that fence building in the UK is restricted by the Town and Country Planning Acts. Normally the rules only apply to fences over 2m (6'6") high, which excludes panel fences. But if the fence is to run along the front of your property and is higher than 1m (3'3"), you must get Planning Permission first.

On a sloping site (below), you can step the fence panels to accommodate changes in level.

DRAWING UP A PLAN

Draw a sketched plan and elevation of the proposed fence, marking on the features described below. Take the plans with you to the suppliers and use as a checklist.

Total length Measure this in metres, then divide by 1.8 to find the number of panels. You'll almost certainly be left with a gap to fill (but don't forget that each post adds 75–100mm), so either adjust the length to the nearest number of whole panels or aim to fill the gap with a cut panel (put this where it is least obvious).

Post positions Work these out from the length of the panels.

Adjoining structures If the fence ends at a house wall or shed, mark this on the plan.

Type of ground Measure and mark on the plan any changes in the type of ground – for example, from bare earth to concrete patio.

Post heights These will be governed by the panel heights, and by the way the posts are anchored (which

in turn could depend on the type of ground). Mark in the heights and anchoring methods for each post. Where a post goes against a house wall, aim to bolt it on using expanding wall anchors (see overleaf).

Caps and gravel boards Mark these on so that you don't forget them.

Fixings etc. List at the side of the plan what fixings are required, including clips, nails, wall anchors and concrete. You'll also need wood preservative for treating the

posts ends and any cut parts.

Tools checklist Aside from the usual woodworking tools, you may need to hire or borrow the following:

■ Post hole borer – for rapid digging of post holes.

■ Sledge hammer – for driving in spiked metal sockets.

■ Hammer drill and 9mm bit – for drilling wall anchor holes.

Sample sketch plans showing the critical measurements and details.

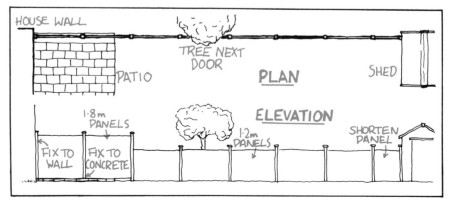

Close boarded panels (left) are the strongest type of panel fence and offer excellent privacy, though their effect can be slightly claustrophobic where space is limited.

Topping plain panels with trellised sections (below) gives extra height and privacy without totally obscuring the view. It also makes an ideal frame for climbing plants.

TYPES OF FENCE PANEL

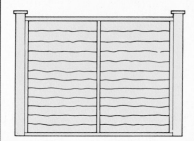

Waney edge panels have overlapping horizontal slats with the bark left on to give a rustic look.

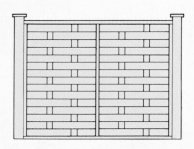

Interwoven panels have horizontal slats with uprights threaded through them. Shrinkage during hot weather can create gaps, reducing privacy.

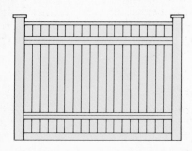

Close (feather) boarded panels have upright overlapping slats fixed to sturdy timber rails. This is the most durable type of panel fence.

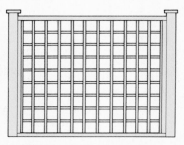

Trellis panels consist of nailed together batten grids. They are an attractive way of sectioning off part of the garden without obscuring the view and make good frames for climbing plants.

PREPARING THE SITE

Clear sites need very little preparation, but if you're using metal spikes, check that there are no electric cables buried along the route. Mains cables and drains are too deep to be affected, but an outdoor supply laid by a previous occupant could be at risk.

Mark the route with string and clear any obstructions.

Old fence posts may be difficult to remove, especially if they are still in reasonable condition. Break up any concrete around the base then push the post from side to side. if it won't pull out, use a timber lever.

Dead hedges should be cut down to about 150mm (6″) above the ground. Dig up the individual stumps and pull them out by hand.

Tree roots could pose problems if they fall exactly where you want a post – standard panel sizes mean the post positions are fixed unless you cut a panel down. Whether you do this or dig up the root may depend on whose tree it is.

1 *Mark out the fence route with string. On a boundary, plan for the posts to be on your side of the line.*

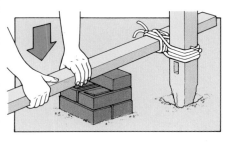

2 *Lever out obstructions such as an old fence post using timber and a pile of bricks. Tie the lever around a large nail knocked into the base of the post.*

PUTTING UP THE FENCE

Put up the fence along your string line, following the sequence shown. By fitting a post, then a panel, then another post, and so on, you ensure that all the panels fit exactly.

If the fence joins a house wall or runs over concrete, use this as your starting point – see *Fixing to Masonry* below right.

Set the rest of the posts in the earth using metal spikes or concrete.

For metal spikes drive them in and fix the posts as you go.

For concreted-in posts, dig the holes and prop the posts upright but don't add the concrete until the run is complete (this allows you to make minor adjustments).

In the meantime, prop the posts upright by packing the holes with pieces of stone or broken brick. If necessary, nail temporary timber props to the posts and remove them after the concrete has set.

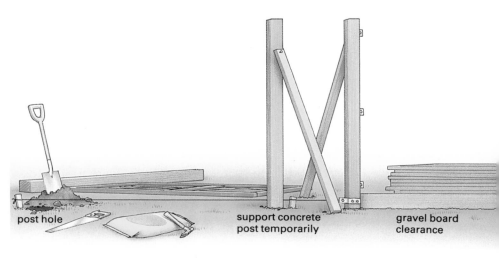

post hole | support concrete post temporarily | gravel board clearance

1 Set the first post, then offer up a panel to check the position of the second post. Set this in place too. Support concreted-in posts temporarily with a length of batten nailed to the top.

2 If you are using gravel boards, test-fit one between the two posts to gauge at what height to fix the panel. Then, if you are using fence clips, nail three to each post at equal intervals.

SETTING THE POSTS

Dig holes for concreted-in posts as you go, allowing an extra 150mm (6″) on top of the sunken depth – 450mm (18″) for fences up to 1.2m (4′) high; 600mm (2′) above this. Use a marked-off stick as shown to check how deep to dig.

Try to keep the sides straight, and no wider than an ordinary garden spade – about 225mm (9″). Pack the bottom 150mm (6″) with compacted rubble to provide a firm base and aid drainage.

Alternatively, hire a post hole borer to make lighter work of the digging. Hand operated ones give good results on all but hard, stony ground.

Before setting a post, soak the ends in a bucket of preservative for at least 10 minutes to provide extra protection against rot. Then lift the post into the hole and pack around

the base with soil and more rubble to within 150mm (6″) of the surface. Ram down with a piece of wood.

When the whole fence is up, fill the holes to the top with a fairly dry coarse concrete mix. Smooth the concrete into a slightly conical shape so that rainwater will run away from the post. Leave for a day before removing any supports.

Metal spikes are simply hammered into the ground wherever you want a post. A wooden driving piece (dolly) that you buy with the spikes protects the heads.

Some makes have a wedge-grip that holds the post firmly. Others have a clamp or bolt which you tighten with the post in place. Normally it's important to get the spike in straight, but some have swivel-mounted heads which can be adjusted to align the post precisely.

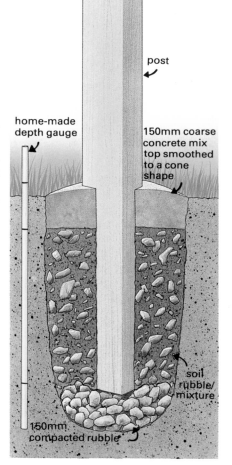

post

home-made depth gauge

150mm coarse concrete mix top smoothed to a cone shape

soil rubble/ mixture

150mm compacted rubble

When bedding a post in concrete, add an extra 150mm (6″) to the depth of the hole and fill this with well compacted rubble. Bed the post itself in a mixture of soil and rubble, then top with a 150mm (6″) layer of coarse concrete. Use a stick to gauge the depth of the various layers.

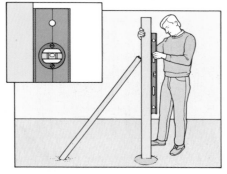

When concreting, use a spirit level to check that the post is vertical. If necessary, nail on a timber support to take the weight while you fix the panels.

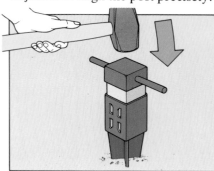

Drive in metal spikes with a sledge hammer, using the wooden dolly supplied. Use the previous panel as a guide to make sure the spike goes in straight.

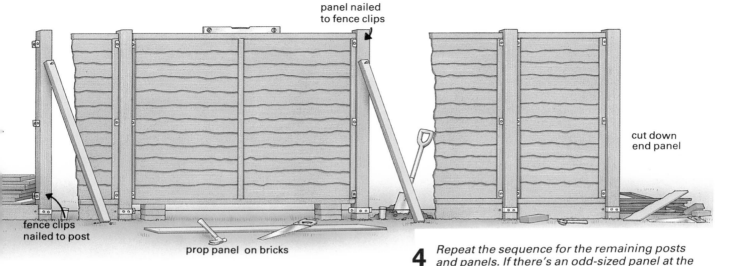

panel nailed
to fence clips

cut down
end panel

fence clips
nailed to post

prop panel on bricks

4 Repeat the sequence for the remaining posts and panels. If there's an odd-sized panel at the end, set the last post in line with the others and cut the panel to fit the space.

3 Prop the panel just above the ground (or gravel board) on bricks or wood. Rest a spirit level on top, check for level, then nail to the fence clips or posts.

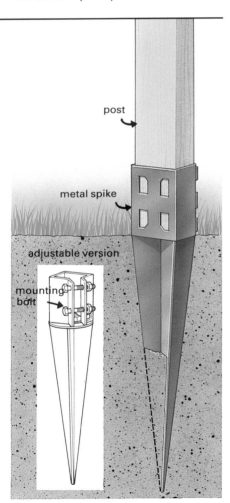

post

metal spike

adjustable version

mounting bolt

Metal post spikes *must be long enough to suit the height of your posts. There are various ways to fix the post in the socket, and some have adjustable tops (inset) so you can correct slight errors in alignment. Fit the post to the clamp, then slacken the bolts to adjust.*

Trade tip

Get a grip on it

❛ *Large panels are difficult to manoeuvre without help because they are wider and taller than a comfortable arm span. I get round the problem by using a length of batten with a large screw in the end: hook this under the panel and use it to take the weight while steadying the top with your other hand.* ❜

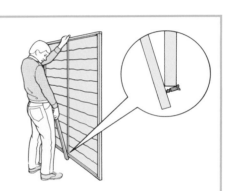

FIXING TO MASONRY

To fit a post in concrete, use a bolt-down socket fastened with expanding wall anchors.

To join to a wall, bolt on the end post with expanding wall anchors. Use three for a post over 1m (3′3″) high. Space them equally and recess the heads into the post. Ensure the post is vertical before marking the holes, and drill into the bricks – not the mortar joints. If the post slants, pack out with wood.

To fit a bolt-down socket, *mark the bolt holes through the fixing plate, then drill. Insert the expanding wall anchors and tighten with a spanner.*

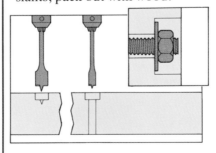

1 To fix to a wall, drill the post at three equal intervals. Enlarge the first 12mm (½″) of each hole so that the bolt heads will be recessed.

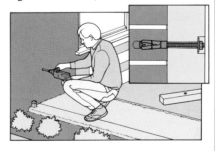

2 Hold the post vertically against the wall, then mark and drill the holes. Tighten the bolts with a car socket spanner, packing behind if necessary.

FIXING THE PANELS

There are two ways to fix the panels to the posts:

Fence clips come in several varieties. Some are U-shaped and are nailed to the posts before slotting in the panels and nailing them in place. Others are nailed to the panels first, then to the posts.

Direct nailing is the alternative, but needs care to avoid splitting the thin battens at the ends of the panel. To be on the safe side, drill pilot holes through the battens first, then nail into the posts.

Fix two clips per side for panels up to 1.2m (4') high, three clips per side for larger panels. Secure them in place with 25mm (1") galvanized nails.

If direct nailing, drill pilot holes first. Use six nails per panel end – three on each side, equally spaced – and nail at a slight angle for extra grip.

FINISHING OFF

■ Often, you need to cut the last panel to fit the remaining space. The easiest way is to prise off the end fixing battens first.

Renail the battens at the new width, then trim off the waste slats and capping strips using a panel saw or jig saw.

■ When the posts are secured, saw the tops to the same height. Cut them square if you are fitting posts caps, otherwise at an angle.

Even on pre-treated timber, cut parts will rapidly deteriorate unless given extra protection. Coat the post tops and any other sawn-off bits with brush-on exterior wood preservative, working it well into the grain.

■ Fix purpose-made post caps with 25mm (1") galvanized nails.

■ If you are fitting gravel boards, fix these to the posts using the special cleats supplied (there are various patterns). Alternatively, nail the boards directly to the posts.

1 To cut down a panel, offer it up to the posts and mark off the width. Then prise off one of the end fixing battens and renail it at the marked point.

2 Prise off the remaining end batten and nail it to the opposite side of the panel. Saw through the surplus slats and capping strips and discard.

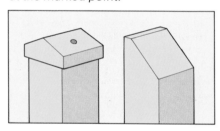

Fix post caps with a pair of nails to stop them twisting.
Alternatively, saw the ends at an angle (to assist water run-off) and coat with preservative.

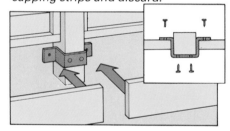

Fix gravel boards using nails or the special cleats supplied. Nail the cleats to the posts first, then slot the boards into place and secure with more nails.

PROBLEM SOLVER

Dealing with slopes

The fixed shape of the panels means that they can't follow the angle of a sloping site. The answer is to step them, and on a slight slope you can do this by eye as you go along. But on a steeper slope, follow this method to get the steps even:

■ Position the first two posts and lay a batten between them with a spirit level on top.

■ Raise the lower end of the batten until it is level, and mark the distance you raised it on an offcut of wood.

■ Cut this offcut to length and use it to mark the height of all the other posts so that they each have the same step.

■ As you fit each panel, excavate any earth which prevents it fitting at the right level. Use this to fill in any low spots elsewhere.

■ Fit gravel boards or bank up the earth in terraces to fill remaining gaps below the panels.

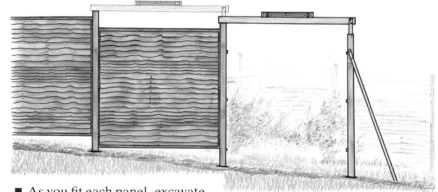

Use an offcut of wood to set the tops of the posts at even steps below each other. Conceal gaps beneath the panels with gravel boards or soil from high spots.

BUILDING A CLOSE-BOARDED FENCE

If you want a wooden fence that's as secure and durable as possible, then the close-boarded type is the best option. This kind of fence is built from scratch, using more substantial timbers than one made from prefabricated panels – so the construction takes rather longer and it may work out a little more expensive. Against this, a close-boarded fence has several advantages:

■ The sturdier boarding should last longer than lightweight panels.
■ It is harder to knock down or climb over.
■ It's easier to adjust the length of the fence and the position of the posts to suit the size of your plot and avoid obstacles such as a tree whose roots straddle the boundary.
■ On sloping ground, you can easily accommodate changes in level.

A close-boarded fence is made by nailing featheredge boards onto a frame of posts and rails – making it easy to vary the design to suit your garden.

....Shopping List....

The materials needed depend on the site (see overleaf) and the construction method used:
Method 1: with rails jointed into posts set in concrete – cheapest, but most work.
Method 2: with rails in metal brackets and posts set in metal spikes – quick, but more costly.
Timber. Use standard sawn posts, arris rails and featheredge boards, sold by timber yards or builder's merchants as well as many DIY superstores and garden centres. For maximum life use timber that has been pre-treated with preservative (this costs about 20% more than untreated wood). Buy extra preservative for treating the post ends and cut sections.
Fixings. For fixing the boards and rails, buy 45mm (1¾") galvanised wire nails. 1kg is enough for about 10m of fence.
Tools checklist: Gardening tools, panel saw, hammer, drill and bits, spirit level, string and pegs, tape measure, chisel (possibly), scrap timber, spike driving dolly (possibly).

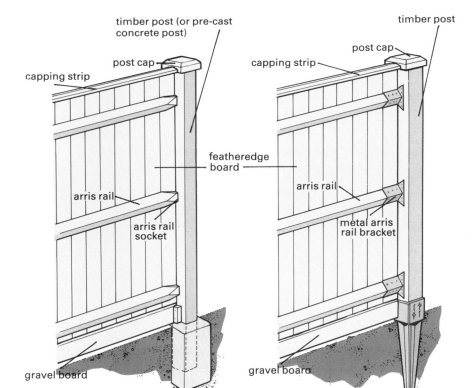

Method 1 construction
- timber post (or pre-cast concrete post)
- post cap
- capping strip
- featheredge board
- arris rail
- arris rail socket
- gravel board
- concrete bedding

Method 2 construction
- timber post
- post cap
- capping strip
- featheredge board
- arris rail
- metal arris rail bracket
- gravel board
- metal post spike

DESIGNING A FENCE

Work out the dimensions of the fence to suit your site and stock timber sizes, then draw up a sketch plan and list of the materials needed.

Deciding the height

Where security is important, the fence should be as tall as possible – but height is the one aspect of putting up a fence which is normally covered by planning regulations. You can normally build a fence up to 2m high (6'6") along a boundary at the back of your property without Planning Permission, but for a fence in front of your property, the maximum height that can be built without Permission is 1m (3'3").

A 2m (6'6") fence is constructed from 1.8m (6') standard lengths of board with a 150mm (6") gravel board along the bottom. For a shorter fence, choose a height which suits standard board lengths. For example, a 1m (3'3") fence can be made from 900mm (3') boards with a 100mm (4") gravel board.

Deciding post positions

Mark out the run of the fence on the site itself using string and pegs.

Allow one post at each end of the fence, one at a corner and one each side of a gate. Elsewhere, the span between posts should be no more than 3m (9'9"), but use 2.4m (8') spans if the fence is regularly subjected to strong winds.

Drive in pegs to show the post positions. If one of these falls awkwardly (eg, next to a prized tree or on a patch of hard ground) there is nothing to stop you moving it so long as the spans are less than the length of an arris rail. If you want the posts at regular intervals, move the others to equalize the spaces.

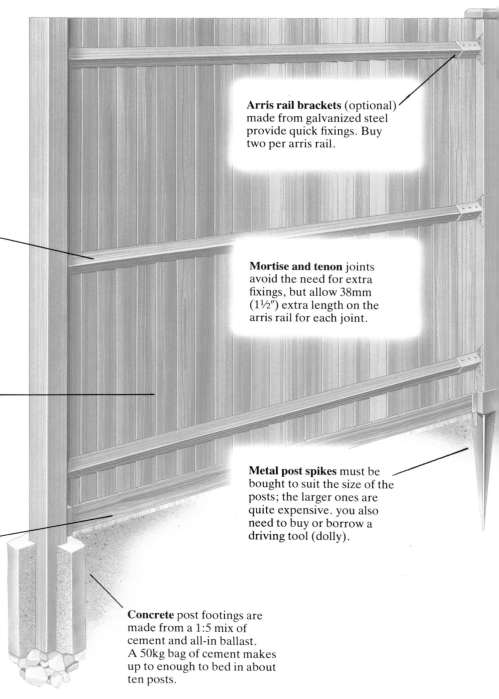

Posts should be about 450mm (18") taller than the height of the fence for bedding in concrete, or the same height if you use metal spikes. Timber posts can be 75 or 100mm (3 or 4") square – use the larger size where security is important, for fences over 1.2m (4') high, where you are hanging a gate in the fence or where there are strong winds. *Pre-cast concrete posts* are more durable and can be bought with ready-made sockets for arris rails.

Arris rails are triangular in section. Use three rails per span for a fence over 1.2m (4') high, but only two rails below this. Standard lengths are 3m (9'9") or 2.4m (8'); adjust your post spacing to suit. If you are jointing the ends into the posts, allow a total of 75mm (3") for the joints, but if you use metal brackets, no allowance is necessary.

Featheredge boards come either 100mm or 150mm (4 or 6") wide in stock lengths of 900mm, 1.2, 1.5, 1.8 and 2.1m (3, 4, 5, 6, 7').

Multiply the total length of the fence in metres by 12.5 (100mm boards) or 7.4 (150mm boards) to get the approximate number needed. It isn't worth deducting the width of the posts from the length of the fence, since you should allow a few boards extra.

Gravel boards fit at the bottom of the fence to stop the ends of the boards touching the ground and rotting. They can be made from 150×25mm (6×1") sawn softwood, fixed in place with lengths of 25×25mm (1×1") batten. Buy the same lengths as the arris rails.

Arris rail brackets (optional) made from galvanized steel provide quick fixings. Buy two per arris rail.

Mortise and tenon joints avoid the need for extra fixings, but allow 38mm (1½") extra length on the arris rail for each joint.

Metal post spikes must be bought to suit the size of the posts; the larger ones are quite expensive. you also need to buy or borrow a driving tool (dolly).

Concrete post footings are made from a 1:5 mix of cement and all-in ballast. A 50kg bag of cement makes up to enough to bed in about ten posts.

Good neighbours

❝ It is normal to put the fence up so that the posts and rails are on your side presenting the 'flush' face of the boards to your neighbour (contrary to popular belief this is not a legal requirement). No part of the fence should be over your boundary line, but make sure your neighbour is aware what you are doing, since you will need to work from both sides. ❞

Capping is optional. Post caps can be bought, or made from scraps of arris rail or gravel board. A capping strip can be fixed to the tops of the boards to protect the end grain from moisture. Buy the same lengths as the arris rails.

DEALING WITH SLOPES

Slopes are easy to deal with because each board is fixed individually and you can arrange for the fence to follow the lie of the land exactly. Position the posts slightly closer together than for a fence on level ground to allow for trimming the gravel boards and rails at an angle.

Set the posts upright, projecting from the ground by the same amount. Fix the arris rails so that they run parallel to the ground. When you come to fix the boards, set their tops against a line fixed between the posts, so that each one steps up or down a fraction from its neighbour.

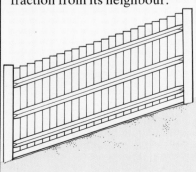

PREPARING THE POSTS AND RAILS

For Method 1 construction, prepare the posts and rails by cutting the mortises and tenons, and treating the wood with preservative. If you are using Method 2 mark the positions of the rails in the same way, as a guide to fixing the brackets.

Preparing the posts

Mark the rail positions on all the posts at once to ensure that they are at the same height:
■ Mark the length of a board on to the posts.
■ For two arris rails, put them about 150mm (6") from the top and bottom of the board. A third rail goes midway between.
■ Separate the posts to mark the mortises individually.
■ Put the mortises about 20mm (¾") from the outside face of the post so the boards are flush.
■ At these positions, mark rectangular mortises 60mm (2½") long and 20mm (¾") wide.

Preparing the rails

Check that the rails are all exactly the same length. To form a tenon, make three saw cuts as shown below. Then treat the ends with preservative.

1 Mark out the rail positions on all the posts together to ensure they are at the same height. Position them according to the height of the boards.

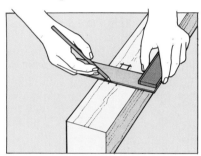

2 Indicate the exact position of each mortise on the posts by drawing a rectangle 60×20mm (2½×¾") set in from the edge of the post by 20mm (¾").

Quick marks

❝ To mark the mortises quickly, make a card template with a hole the right size, folded to fit over the edge of the post. ❞

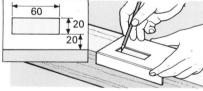

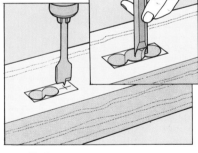

3 Drill out the bulk of the wood by making a series of holes using a 20mm (¾") drill bit. Finish off the mortise by chiselling it square.

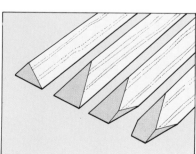

Cut tenons at both ends of the arris rails by making three saw cuts. Test fit into your mortises and chisel off some wood if the joints are tight.

Brush or spray preservative liberally over all holes and cuts. Stand the base of each post in preservative, allowing it at least ten minutes to soak in.

PUTTING UP THE FRAME: METHOD 1

Put up the framework of the fence by assembling the posts and rails working along from one end. Use your string line as a guide to the run of the fence and drive in pegs to indicate post positions.

■ Dig the post holes at the pegs.

■ Set in the first post, propping it and packing hardcore around the base to keep it upright.

■ Stand the second post loosely in place and fit rails between the two.

■ Prop the second post upright and make sure that the rails are level (except where you are following a slope). Raise or lower one post to adjust.

■ Carry on in this way until the framework is complete.

■ Pack concrete (a 1:5 mix of cement and all-in aggregate) around the base of each post and leave it to cure before nailing on the boards.

1 Dig the post holes as square as possible, about 250–300mm (10–12") across and 600mm (24") deep. Fill the bottom 150mm (6") with hardcore. Prop the first post upright ensuring it is square to the line of the fence.

2 Stand the second post in place, set the rails in their mortises and prop the post. Check that the rails are horizontal and that the post is upright.

3 When all posts and rails are in place, fill each post hole with concrete to slightly above ground level. Shape the concrete to slope away from the post.

Trade tip

The last post

❝ If you are using mortise joints and the last post is butted tightly up to an obstacle, you may have difficulty in fitting the rails into the holes in the posts. In this case, saw the rails off square and fasten them using galvanized steel arris rail brackets. ❞

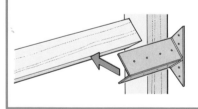

PUTTING UP THE FRAME: METHOD 2

Following your string line, set the posts in one by one guided by the peg positions – but use the arris rails to check the spacing of the posts.

■ Drive in the first post spike using the dolly and a sledge hammer.

■ Set the first post in place checking that it is upright. Some sockets hold the post with barbs, others need screws to secure it.

■ Check the spacing of the second post using an arris rail and fix this post in position using a metal post spike in the same way.

■ Fix the rails between the posts using galvanized arris rail brackets.

■ Carry on in this way until the frame is complete.

1 Drive in the metal spike and fix the first post in position. Use a spirit level to ensure that the spike is driven in straight and that the post is upright.

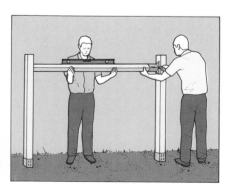

2 Use an arris rail to fix the position of the second post. Screw or nail the rails in place using metal brackets while a helper holds them level.

FIXING THE BOARDS

If the posts are set in concrete, allow this to harden for as long as possible (a day at least) before nailing on the boards. If you don't the posts may work loose.

Boarding is a quick and simple process, made simpler by making a spacing gauge from an offcut cut to the width of a board less 12mm (½"). Use this to set each board overlapping its neighbour by the same amount. The only other point to watch is that the tops of all the boards are level (minor variations at the base are hidden by the gravel board).

1 Nail a batten or stretch a string tightly between the pair of posts you are working on, to act as a guide to setting the boards level.

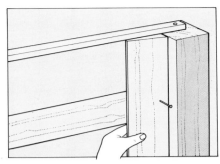

2 Fit the first board with its thick edge butted up to the post. Drive one nail into the middle of each arris rail through the thick part of the board.

3 Use an offcut cut to the width of a board less 12mm (½") to set the next board overlapping the first one by the right amount. Set subsequent boards in same way.

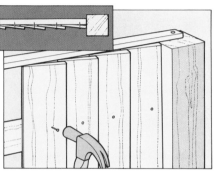

4 Nail each board making sure the nails do not go through the previous one as this would prevent them from moving when they shrink or expand.

5 As you near the post, test-fit the last few boards. Continuing the standard laying pattern may leave an unequal gap when you reach the last board.

6 One alternative is to close up the gaps between the last three or four boards to take up the difference gradually. Nail the last board in the usual way, then drive extra nails through the thin edge as well.

Trade tip

Finishing the end

❝ If you prefer not to vary the spacing of the boards to fit the space, continue laying them in the standard pattern. When you are left with a gap too small to fill, reverse the last board and fit it with the thick edge towards the post. ❞

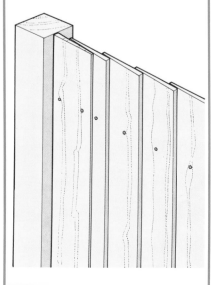

FIXING GRAVEL BOARDS AND CAPPING

Capping is optional, but does ensure maximum weatherproofing and longer life. There are two alternative ways to cap the fence:

■ Fit separate post caps and nail capping strips to the tops of the boards.

■ Run wide capping strips continuously along the top so that these cover the tops of the posts as well as the fence boards.

Gravel boards should always be fitted. You can use metal brackets for fixing them to the posts (essential if using concrete posts) or battens, which are quick, and cheap to buy.

1 **Run continuous capping** across the tops of posts and boards. Nail the ends and a few points between into the thick parts of the boards.

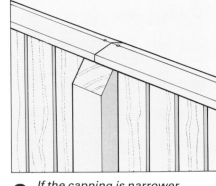

2 If the capping is narrower than the posts, saw the tops of the posts off at an angle as shown to help them shed rainwater.

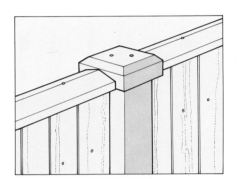

Alternatively, nail post caps to the top of each post. Cut lengths of capping strip and nail them to the tops of the boards at a few points along the fence.

Trade tip

Avoiding splits

❝ If the nails tend to split the boards, drill a small hole through the capping and the top of the board and nail through. ❞

Nail gravel boards to lengths of batten, then nail the battens to the posts so that the boards are flush up to the back of the featheredge boarding.

PROBLEM SOLVER

Arris rails too short

If you make a mistake when setting out the posts you may end with a gap which is too large to span with a single arris rail of the maximum length available. Ideally, you should reset the post, but as this is not always possible, the alternative is to use a galvanized steel repair bracket. Saw the arris rail short at a convenient point and join it to a second section by nailing on the repair bracket. Then fit the extended rail to the posts as normal.

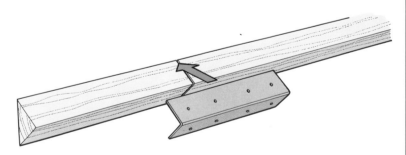

Lengthen an arris rail by using a metal repair bracket to splice on a new section. Then fit it to the posts in the normal way.

Fitting round a tree

Where a tree straddles the fence you can fit round it by putting posts as close as possible on each side and stopping the fence short.

If a tree is growing at an angle so it only partly breaks through the fence, position arris rails across wherever possible and nail on boards shortened to fit.

Fit over tree roots by raising the bottom rail and fitting shorter boards. Support the gravel board on pegs each side.

HANGING ENTRANCE GATES

Gates may be used for purely decorative reasons or to provide essential security.

■ Front gates are mainly decorative, but as they are in constant use and subject to heavy wear, must still be well made and securely hung.

■ Side gates are normally intended to keep out intruders and need to be about 2m (6′6″) high. They should be sturdily made – ideally with vertical boards to make them hard to climb – and securely fastened.

■ Drive gates are wide and heavy, requiring very sturdy posts and room to swing. Fitting a pair of half-width gates may be a way to minimize both these problems.

If you are building a new fence or wall, include any necessary gates at the earliest stage of your plans: it is usually far easier to adapt the fence or wall to suit a standard gate than to make a gate fit a non-standard opening.

If you are replacing a gate, or fitting one where none previously existed, the techniques for hanging are the same but you may need to have the gate made specially to fit the space.

Fence systems often include matching gates, making it easy to include one in the design. You may also need to hang a gate in place of a damaged old one, or to secure an open entrance.

....Shopping List....

Gates are sold by garden centres, builders merchants, DIY stores and timber yards in a limited range of stock sizes. Common examples are:
■ 1067×915mm (3′6″×3′)
■ 1067×1067mm (3′6″×3′6″)
■ 1219×1067mm (4′×3′6″)
■ 1830×915mm (6′×3′)
Non-standard gates can be made to order (see Problem Solver).
Finish Most gates are made from softwood pre-treated with preservative to prevent rotting – if not, apply preservative before hanging. For a gate in a fence, this should be sufficient (use a *coloured preservative* to match).

Otherwise, use a *microporous stain* for a natural wood finish. A traditional painted finish must be applied to full exterior standards – primer, undercoat, topcoat – or you can use a microporous system.
Hinges These depend on how the gate is hung (see overleaf). Choose *strap hinges* for a lightweight gate, or *T hinges* where there is less room on one side. For heavier gates use cast-iron *reversible strap hinges* or a *hook and pin set*. Many of these are galvanized – if not, paint to resist rusting.
Catches, locks and bolts vary to suit the situation. For a wider selection, visit an architectural ironmonger.
Tools checklist: Drill and bits, screwdriver, plane (maybe), saw (maybe), painting tools.

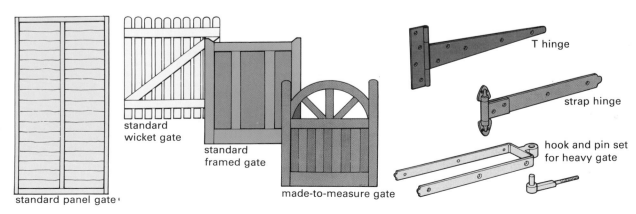

standard panel gate

standard wicket gate

standard framed gate

made-to-measure gate

T hinge

strap hinge

hook and pin set for heavy gate

CHOOSING AND FITTING

Choose a style of gate to suit both the house and the wall or fence you are fitting it to.

If you are replacing an old gate or hanging it in an existing opening, the size will be fixed. If you are building a wall or fence at the same time, choose a convenient size of gate and design around it.

Hanging direction Many types of gate are designed only to be viewed from one side. They are also often made for right or left hand hanging; if there are diagonal braces, these should run upwards from the hinge side, while the timber on the hinge side may be thicker than on the catch side. Double gates need to be fitted as a matched pair.

Height A full-height gate should be about 50mm (2″) shorter than the wall or fence to allow plenty of clearance at the base.

Width Where the posts are fixed, the choice of hanging method dictates the width:

■ Flush with one face, using flush fitting hinges and catches. The gate needs to be about 12mm (½″) narrower than the gap between the posts and will only open one way.

■ On the face of the posts, using cranked hinges or hook and pin sets. The gate should be at least 25mm (1″) wider than the gap between the posts and will only open one way. It will be hard to secure too.

■ Between the posts, centred so the gate swings either way. This needs a large clearance – as much as 150mm (6″) depending on the design – and again makes the gate hard to secure.

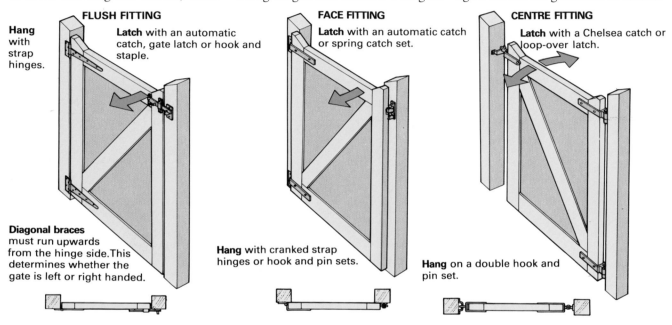

FLUSH FITTING

Hang with strap hinges.

Latch with an automatic catch, gate latch or hook and staple.

Diagonal braces must run upwards from the hinge side. This determines whether the gate is left or right handed.

FACE FITTING

Latch with an automatic catch or spring catch set.

Hang with cranked strap hinges or hook and pin sets.

CENTRE FITTING

Latch with a Chelsea catch or loop-over latch.

Hang on a double hook and pin set.

The opening direction and the way the gate is fitted to the posts affects what type of gate, hinges and catches or bolts you buy.

BUYING GATES TO FIT

If you're hanging a gate in an opening where a stock one won't fit, there are three options:

■ Have a gate made to size. This can be done to order by many of the stockists who supply standard gates, by specialist gate manufacturers, or by a local joinery workshop. It may well prove expensive, but is the only realistic option if you want a decorative entrance gate or a very large and heavy gate – for a vehicle entrance, say.

■ Adapt the opening to take a standard gate. For example, if the opening is wider than standard, you could fit extra posts on either side to take up the difference and hang a gate from that (see page 68).

■ Make a gate to the exact size needed. Although large ones are beyond DIY, it is by no means hard or expensive to construct a utility-style gate (see Problem Solver).

Non-standard decorative gates can be made to order in many styles, or to match a traditional design as here – get a quote from a gate specialist or joinery workshop.

FITTING POSTS

Gates can be hung on firm wooden posts as well as on solid masonry. Where no posts are in place, or where the existing ones are unsuitable, simply fit new ones.

Unsuitable posts include thin wooden ones – 75×75mm (3×3″) is normally the minimum for even a lightweight gate, rising to 100×100mm (4×4″) for a taller, heavier one. Wide gates across a drive may need 150×150mm (6×6″) or even 200×200mm (8×8″) posts. Beware of hanging a gate from a post which is fixed using a metal post spike as this may not be strong enough. Even for a light gate, a firm concrete bedding is more reliable.

Fitting new posts

For lightweight gates, just bed wooden posts in concrete to a depth of about 450mm (18″). For a heavier gate, set them deeper – 600mm (2′) or more – and form a trench linking the two posts so that they are both set in a single block of concrete rather than two separate ones.

Use the gate to fix the spacing of the posts and nail on temporary braces to hold them in position until the concrete has set – allow it to harden for about a week before hanging the gate.

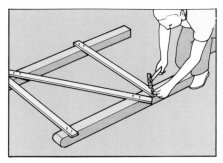

1 Lay the posts down and use the gate to fix the spacing. Leaving any necessary clearance gap, nail two battens across and add a third batten diagonally to keep the posts in line.

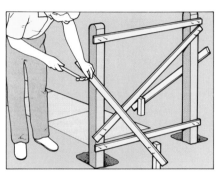

3 Set the posts upright and level. Pack with hardcore and prop with battens, then shovel in concrete and tamp down well. If you dug a trench, this now forms a concrete 'bridge'.

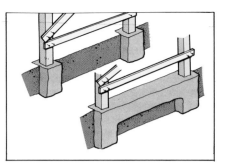

2 For a light gate, dig two post holes about 300mm (12″) square and 450mm (18″) deep. For a heavy gate dig them 600mm (2′) deep and join with a trench about 300mm (12″) square.

Trade tip

Extra bracing

6 To help prevent a post from sagging, bolt a stout cross member to it, then embed the whole lot in concrete. The cross piece helps to spread the load of the gate. 9

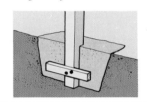

HINGING THE GATE

If you are fitting a gate between a new pair of posts, they should have been set at the right spacing. Where you are hanging a gate on existing posts, it may need trimming unless it was made to measure.

Depending on your hanging method, try the gate in place, allowing for the thickness of the hinges you are using. If necessary, trim with a plane.

With timber posts, screw the hinges to the gate first, then prop it in place and mark the hinge positions on the posts ready for fixing. The hinges may bolt or screw to the post, depending on their design. Check the alignment, and the ground clearance for the full swing, before inserting all the screws.

With masonry posts which have existing pins mortared in, use these for the new hinges if you can, and position the gate hinges to match.

If there are no existing hinge pins or they are badly rusted, it may prove tricky to fit new hinges to the existing masonry. If you have to do so, see Problem Solver for details of the options.

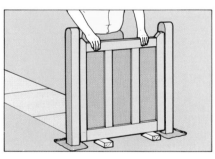

1 Test the gate in place, propping it on wooden blocks to leave clearance at the base. Plane the edges to leave a fitting clearance if necessary.

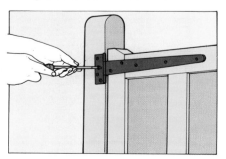

2 Fit the hinges to the gate and align it between the posts. Fix with one or two screws to check that it works properly, then add the remaining screws.

Trade tip

Stopping dropping

6 Large, heavy gates are prone to sag as the hinges wear and the frame settles. This is difficult to prevent, so allow for it by temporarily nailing small blocks of wood to the upper and lower edge of the gate, then hang it in the ordinary way. The blocks ensure that the gate is slightly tilted to counteract any sagging which may occur. 9

Fixing to a masonry post

Fitting hinges to a masonry post or wall can be difficult. If the hinges are designed for screw fitting, it is hard to fix them securely in proper alignment. And if they are designed to be mortared in, this too can prove difficult unless the wall is built at the same time.

An easier option in many cases is to bolt or screw a sturdy piece of timber to the masonry using fixing brackets and masonry anchor bolts, then fix to this as you would to an ordinary wooden post.

In any case, you should ensure that the masonry is strong enough to take the weight. A separate pier should be a minimum of 300mm (12") square and must be built on a firm foundation. Don't fix any nearer than about 100mm (4") from the corner of a house.

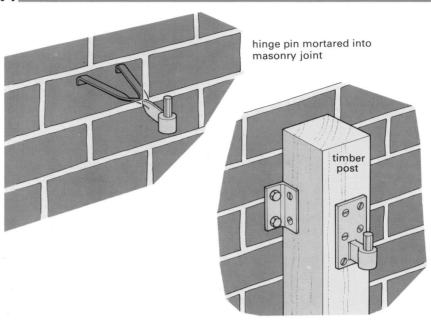

hinge pin mortared into masonry joint

timber post

Fixing to masonry: masonry hinge pins are designed to be mortared in and are difficult to add after the wall has been built. As an alternative, fix a wooden post against the masonry and then hang the gate on that.

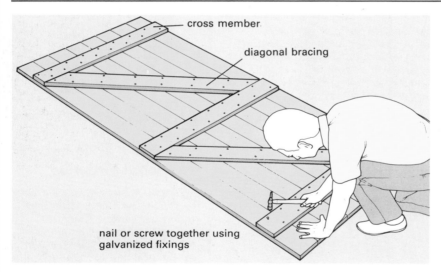

cross member

diagonal bracing

nail or screw together using galvanized fixings

Basic construction: For a small gate a single 'Z' frame is sufficient – taller ones need two. Make the panelling from sawn softwood, featheredge boards or tongued and grooved board, treated with preservative.

Making a DIY gate

A basic boarded gate is fairly easy to make. It consists of a sturdy cross frame with diagonal braces on to which the panelling is fixed. For a gate in a panel fence, the panelling can be made of standard sawn softwood; use featheredge boards for a close-boarded style fence. For a more finished gate to hang in brickwork, use tongued and grooved softwood panelling.

■ Cut the cross members from 100×25mm (4×1") timber. For a half-height gate you only need two – for a full-height gate use three.

■ Cut the panels to the same length and lay the cross timbers on them at right angles. Nail or screw in place.

■ Making sure the gate is square, cut the diagonal braces to fit exactly between the cross timbers. Nail or screw them in place to make a rigid structure.

Afterwards, hang the gate in the conventional way using strap hinges attached to the cross members; ensure that the braces run upwards from the hinge side. Fit the catch to the end of the upper (or centre) cross member, not the boards.

Treat with timber preservative and finish as required.

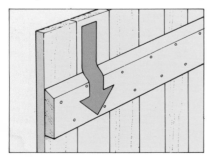

Refinement 1: Plane off the top edges of the cross members as shown so that they shed water rather than trap it and encourage rot to develop.

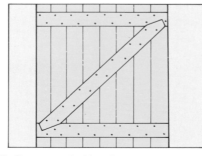

Refinement 2: Notch the cross members as shown by making two saw cuts. Cut the diagonal braces to fit so that they are securely locked in place.

PUTTING UP A GARDEN SHED

Even in a small garden, a shed is a virtual necessity for storing tools or odds and ends. You could build one from scratch, or opt for a concrete mini-garage, but the easiest – and often the cheapest – solution is to construct it from a prefabricated wooden kit.

Shed kits are sold mail order from the manufacturer, and by garden centres, timber merchants, superstores and specialist dealers.

The sheds themselves range in size from compact 'sentry boxes' to much larger 'summer house' styles, but assembly is much the same in all cases. After some straightforward site preparation, you simply fasten the prefabricated panels together, cover the roof with nail-on felt, and fit out the interior.

Types of kit

Panel-construction kits are available in a range of styles, including *heavy duty* sheds which double as workshops or potting sheds. You decide on the size and shape you want – and sometimes the positions of the door and windows too – then order the shed as a complete package which includes finished panels.

Modular 'flat-pack' kits are made up from wall, door and window panels in standard sizes. These are more versatile as they combine in various ways to produce different sizes and styles of shed.

Modular sheds are made up of standard size panels so they can be tailored to suit any garden simply by swapping the positions of the windows and door and adding extension packs.

.... Shopping List ....

Panel construction sheds come as a complete kit with ready-built wall, floor and roof sections; with larger models the sections may be in two or more parts. Windows are either pre-fitted, or the glass is supplied loose with glazing battens. The doors come separately with their hinges and a bolt or padlock hasp. Roofing felt is supplied loose.

Modular sheds come in packs – the bigger the shed the more packs you need. A small shed will consist of two end packs which typically include wall, floor, roof, door and window sections. To increase the shed size buy **extension packs** containing extra wall, floor and roof sections.

Site preparation In all cases you will need preservative-treated *timber bearers* to support the shed off the ground. These may not come with the kit but can usually be bought as an extra. Alternatively, buy pre-treated (eg Tanalised) timber and cut it to length. Small sheds need 75×75mm (3×3″) bearers, large or heavy duty sheds 100×100mm (4×4″) ones. Allow at least one bearer for every 600mm (24″) length of shed.

Bricks or *concrete blocks* may also be needed to raise the bearers off the ground if this tends to get waterlogged. *Paving slabs* or *concrete* are only required if you decide to lay your shed on a solid base (see overleaf).

Preservative treatment is usually applied at the factory, but it does no harm to apply an extra coat – some shed manufacturers recommend you use a spirit-based preservative, *not* a water-based one. As a rough guide allow 2.5 litres for a shed up to 2.4×1.8m (8×6′).

Extra fittings include hardboard and fibreglass or polystyrene foam insulation for lining the shed, shelves, workbenches and materials for running in an electricity supply.

Tools checklist: Screwdrivers, spanner for coach bolts, hammer, trimming knife, gardening tools and weedkiller for site preparation.

CHOOSING A SHED

The first step is deciding where to put the shed. You don't need planning permission for an ordinary kit so long as it won't be in front of the Building Line and is at least 1m (39″) from the boundary.

In most cases a shed goes best in a corner of the garden, though if you intend to use it as a workshop you should make sure the site isn't too dingy.

With a site in mind, check through suppliers' catalogues and go for the biggest shed you can fit in – storage space quickly gets used up.

Assessing the options

For any given style and size of shed, there is unlikely to be much choice either of material or constructional method (for the variations, see *Shed construction* opposite). However, doors, windows and interior fittings may present a number of options – see opposite – so consider these before making a firm decision.

Where to buy from

Garden centres and specialist retailers often have display sites where you can examine the different types of shed and check on the construction quality. You generally have to order the model you want; delivery times may range from 'next day' where stocks are held on site, to several weeks if the order has to be forwarded to the manufacturer.

DIY superstores normally carry a limited range of either panel construction or modular sheds, but may not display them assembled for you to examine.

You can also buy sheds by mail order direct from the makers. They will supply catalogues, but it can be hard to assess quality this way.

STYLES OF SHED

Pitched roof (also called *Apex*) sheds are the traditional design, with the roof rising from the sides to a central ridge. This arrangement gives good headroom in the centre but less at the sides.

Flat roof sheds are virtually the same height all round, though the roof has a slight fall to let water run off.
Pent roof sheds are simply flat roof designs with the roof panel at a steeper angle; the roof slopes up from the back or side of the shed to the front. This design is good for workshops since it offers reasonable headroom at the front – where the workbench is normally fitted.

Solar front sheds are a variation on the flat/pent roof theme, with the front wall of the shed angled outwards. The windows form the top section of the front and let in plenty of light – very useful in a potting shed. Solar front sheds usually come complete with a full-length slatted workbench which runs under the windows and so doesn't take up any of the main floor area – a useful space saver.

SHED OPTIONS

Doors in pent/flat roofed sheds can go in the end or side walls; an end position makes it easier to get in ladders or bikes, and also allows for a full-length workbench. Pitched roof sheds have the door in one end.

Double doors are an option on larger sheds, giving better access for mowers, barrows or other bulky equipment. *Stable doors* (where the top half can be opened independently of the bottom) are also available.

On panel construction sheds, say exactly where you want the door when ordering. Modular sheds allow for fitting in any position.

Windows are essential for both light and ventilation if you plan to work in the shed.

Most sheds come with fixed windows as standard; opening ones (hinged or louvred) usually cost extra but are worth it for the extra ventilation. Both types fit a standard opening in the side of the shed. Not all windows are glass: cheaper kits use acrylic sheet, and some leave the glazing to you.

Workbenches often come with the shed (especially if it's a solar front design) or are available as an optional extra. Most are designed to fit along the wall under the window. They may be free-standing, or else held to the shed frame by brackets at the rear and legs at the front.

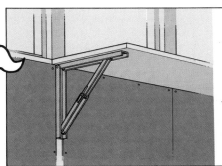

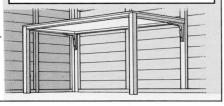

SHED CONSTRUCTION

Garden shed kits are all made up from a series of panels, the walls consisting of *cladding planks* nailed to a timber framework.

Two main types of cladding are used: *shiplap*, in which the planks are tongued and grooved into one another; and *overlap*, where each plank overlaps the one below. Overlap cladding is generally the less costly of the two, but also tends to be less weather-resistant.

Heavy-duty sheds cost about half as much again as comparable standard types. For this you get more substantial frame members, thicker cladding and a stronger floor; there may also be a lining of building paper fitted between the cladding and the frame to prevent draughts and rain penetration.

Cladding materials

The less expensive shed kits use a light-coloured cladding such as *pine* or *deal*. These woods are prone to

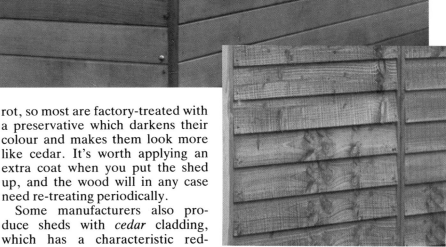

rot, so most are factory-treated with a preservative which darkens their colour and makes them look more like cedar. It's worth applying an extra coat when you put the shed up, and the wood will in any case need re-treating periodically.

Some manufacturers also produce sheds with *cedar* cladding, which has a characteristic red-brown colour. Cedar is naturally resistant to decay, so doesn't need treating, but is more expensive.

Shiplap cladding in red cedar (top) and overlap cladding in larch (above).

PUTTING UP A SHED

The site must be prepared before the shed arrives. Normally, this simply involves levelling it and making sure the surface is firm. But sites that slope, or where space is restricted, need special consideration – see Problem Solver.

Positioning the bearers

Treated timber bearers are used to raise the shed floor off the ground, reducing the risk of damp attacking the woodwork and causing decay. The bearers must sit on a firm base or the shed will be unstable, and there are three ways to arrange this:

■ The simplest method – more than adequate in most cases – is to lay the bearers directly on the ground. Remove any grass or vegetation first, then level and firm the site with a roller. Treat the base area with a long-lasting weedkiller such as sodium chlorate (take care where you spray as it kills everything!) before you start construction.

■ For added protection, or where the ground is waterlogged, raise the bearers off the ground on bricks or concrete blocks positioned at 600mm (2′) intervals (400mm (16″) if the floor will be heavily loaded).

■ For extra firm support with a large shed (but not on waterlogged ground), lay the bearers on a solid concrete slab or on paving slabs bedded in sand and cement mortar.

Position the bearers on the prepared site (above). Check that they are at the required spacing, set level, and squared up ready to take the floor panels.

Large sheds are best supported on a base made up of paving slabs (below). Make sure all the slabs are level before laying the bearers in position.

FITTING THE ROOF

With the walls firmly fixed and square to one another, fit the roof panels – they screw or nail to brackets on the top frame members.

The bare panels are covered with overlapping strips of felt, nailed in place and trimmed at the eaves. Some kits include battens and fascia boards for finishing the edges.

---Trade tip---

Lining up

❝ Throughout assembly, you'll find that even a minor misalignment between sections will stop you sliding in the bolts. I fit a sturdy crosshead screwdriver through one of the bolt holes and use it to lever the corresponding hole into line. ❞

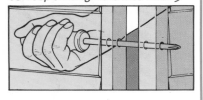

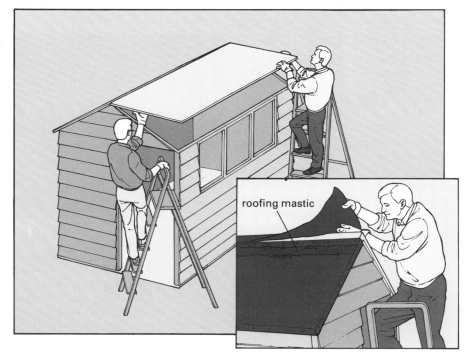

roofing mastic

1 Fit mounting brackets to the walls and lift the roof panels into place. Square the panels up to the walls, then attach to the brackets and along the eaves.

2 Lay on the roofing felt, allowing generous overlaps between the strips and at the edges. Nail the felt in place, then fit any trim boards.

ASSEMBLING THE KIT

Undo the packs, identify each of the sections, and check which goes where – for example, several may have to be fitted together to form a side. Pay particular attention to the positions of the doors and windows.

Panel construction shed sections are large and unwieldy, so you'll need at least a couple of helpers. The panels for modular sheds are generally easier to handle, but an extra pair of hands is helpful when lining up the bolt holes.

Assembling the sections

The walls are built up on the floor and secured with nails or screws through the bottom frame members. Where a wall is made up of more than one section fit them one at a time, starting with a corner.

■ Joints between sections are usually made with coach bolts through pre-drilled holes in the side frame members. Fit washers over the threaded ends, followed by the nuts, and tighten.

■ Alternatively, you may find that large screws are supplied. Fit them through the pre-drilled and countersunk holes in one side frame member so that they screw into the adjoining member on the next. If there are no pilot holes, drill your own after lining the sections up; this stops the frame splitting.

Trade tip

Delivery checks

❝ Shed panels are pretty big, so most suppliers will deliver them (often for free if you live within a few miles). Before you sign the delivery note, check that the panels are not damaged – you don't want to get halfway through the job to find this.

Also, think about how to get the panels to the site – if you haven't got access down the side of the house, and they are too big to go through the front door, you may have to get them over the garden wall! ❞

1 *Stand the floor on its edge by the ends of the bearers, lower it down on to them and slide into position. Skew-nail separate sections of floor together.*

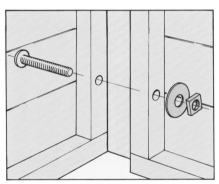

2 *Lift an end wall into position and secure it to the floor. With a helper steadying it, position the back wall so the pre-drilled fixing holes align.*

3 *Insert the fixings and tighten to draw the two walls together, then fasten the second wall to the floor. Repeat this sequence for the other end, then the front.*

DOOR AND WINDOWS

The door can usually be hung so that it opens either side – pick the one where it's least in the way.

If the window glass is supplied loose, it is held in place in the window aperture with nails, triangular nails (called *sprigs*) or strips of wood (glazing strips).

To make the windows completely weatherproof run a bead of linseed oil putty or frame sealing mastic around the aperture before fitting the glass.

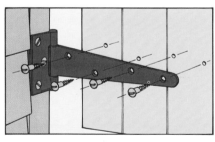

Screw the door hinges to the side of the opening, hold the door in position and fit a couple of mounting screws. Check the action and complete the fitting.

Trade tip

Making doors secure

❝ The door hinges and the lock or hasp are usually supplied with screws to hold them on, but this isn't very secure – any would-be thief can have the door off in a couple of minutes. You can make things more difficult for intruders by fastening the hinges and hasps using security screws or coach bolts – they can't be undone from the outside. ❞

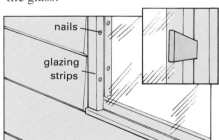

Fixed windows *are held by glazing strips or sprigs (inset). Get a helper to hold the pane of glass in position and nail the strips in place with panel pins.*

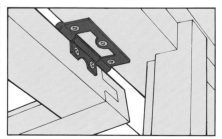

Opening windows *With someone holding the window mark the hole positions, fit one screw each side and check the window closes. Then fit the remaining screws.*

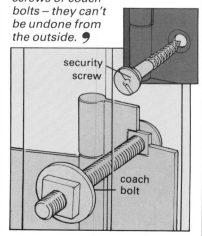

security screw

coach bolt

LINING AND FITTING OUT

Fitting out the shed before you use it will pay dividends later, particularly with regard to storage for tools and garden clutter. Save money by using utility brackets and sawn timber to make rough shelves.

If you plan to work in the shed, it's worth taking the fitting-out a stage further – insulation, lined walls and a decent workbench are all essential.

A mains power supply will also prove invaluable. You could get an electrician to run a circuit cable from the house to a terminal in the shed, then take care of the light and socket wiring yourself.

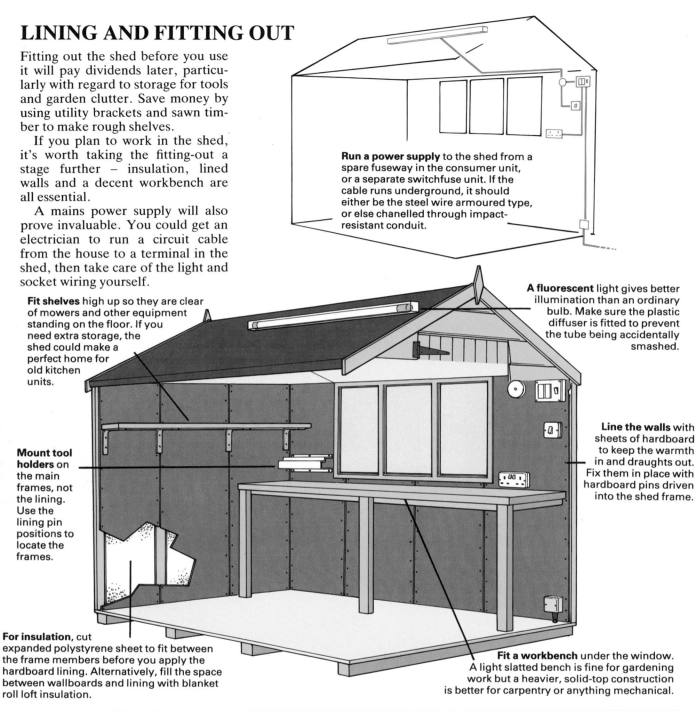

Run a power supply to the shed from a spare fuseway in the consumer unit, or a separate switchfuse unit. If the cable runs underground, it should either be the steel wire armoured type, or else chanelled through impact-resistant conduit.

Fit shelves high up so they are clear of mowers and other equipment standing on the floor. If you need extra storage, the shed could make a perfect home for old kitchen units.

A fluorescent light gives better illumination than an ordinary bulb. Make sure the plastic diffuser is fitted to prevent the tube being accidentally smashed.

Mount tool holders on the main frames, not the lining. Use the lining pin positions to locate the frames.

Line the walls with sheets of hardboard to keep the warmth in and draughts out. Fix them in place with hardboard pins driven into the shed frame.

For insulation, cut expanded polystyrene sheet to fit between the frame members before you apply the hardboard lining. Alternatively, fill the space between wallboards and lining with blanket roll loft insulation.

Fit a workbench under the window. A light slatted bench is fine for gardening work but a heavier, solid-top construction is better for carpentry or anything mechanical.

PROBLEM SOLVER

Sloping sites

Ideally, a sloping site should be levelled by digging up part of it and dispersing the spoil behind a retaining wall to level the rest. In this case, compact the spoil as you go to stop it settling later.

Another, often easier, solution is to build a series of pillars to support the shed bearers every 400–600mm (16–24″). Dig down to firm sub-soil and cast a 300×300mm (12×12″) square concrete base for each pillar, then build the pillars themselves from bricks or concrete blocks. Make sure that the tops are level and the sides vertical.

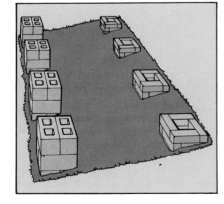

On a sloping site, you can raise the shed off the ground on bricks or concete blocks.

No room to move

Where the shed has to go close to a fence, your manoeuvring room may be limited.

With some types of modular shed, the answer is simply to lay the floor in position and then work from the inside.

But with other designs, you may have to assemble the shed some distance from the site and then manoeuvre it on to the bearers by hand – a job for which you'll probably need some assistance. With the shed in position, double-check that none of the fixings have loosened up during moving.

ADDING A CONSERVATORY

A conservatory can be a relatively inexpensive way to add extra living space or provide room for growing plants. But as with most add-on constructions, it pays to consider the options carefully before committing yourself to what could still prove a major investment.

Conservatories first became popular in the Victorian era for displaying the rare and sub-tropical plants which were then in fashion. More recently – and often under the title of 'sun lounge' – they have made a comeback as a simple way of adding extra living space.

While still an ideal place to grow plants, a modern conservatory can provide a place to sit out, a playroom for children, a dining area, or a utility room. And if properly designed and built, it should form a natural link between the house and garden which allows you to enjoy both at once.

What is a conservatory?
A conservatory is essentially a greenhouse attached to the house, and like most greenhouses it consists almost entirely of glass. This not only makes it extremely light and airy but also very warm – the 'greenhouse effect', familiar to anyone who leaves a car in the sun with the windows closed, produces much higher temperatures inside than outside whenever the sun is shining.

The result is that you can sit in a conservatory virtually all year round when the sun is out, even if the temperature outside is low. Conservatories also provide a considerable degree of insulation and draughtproofing for the rooms to which they are attached

Choosing a site
To make the most of the conservatory, it should be sited where it will get most sun. In the northern hemisphere, this means south-facing, or as close to south as possible.

Avoid a site which is shaded by other buildings, or which is under or close to trees; not only is there a danger of damage from falling branches but many trees, especially limes, produce a sticky substance which makes cleaning the glass a frequent· and unpleasant job. You should also take into account the positions of drains, downpipes and

ventilators or flue outlets – it pays to avoid them if possible.

Where building in front of an airbrick or vent is unavoidable, a duct must be installed in the concrete slab which will form the base of the new conservatory. A manhole cover can also be built over by replacing it with a special double sealed cover, but you should inform the local Building Control Office first, irrespective of any other regulations that may apply.

Rules and regulations
As with any major alteration, adding a conservatory may involve two sets of rules – the Planning Acts and the Building Regulations.
In England and Wales, conservatories follow the same planning rules as extensions – in other words, you are allowed a certain amount of 'permitted development' without any red tape. If the conservatory is going on the back or side of the house, and you don't already have an extension, it is unlikely to require planning permission. Even so, it's

A well-planned conservatory enables you to make the most of your garden. It also provides welcome extra living space on all but very cold or wet days. Look out for labour-saving finishes, like this aluminium frame.

important to check with your local authority's Planning Department at an early stage.

Conservatories are also exempt from the Building Regulations providing they have a roof made from transparent or translucent material (such as glass, acrylic or polycarbonate) and are no more than 30sq m (322sq ft) in area.
In Scotland, conservatories do require planning permission, and they must also abide by the Scottish Building Regulations.

Types of conservatory
Conservatories come in many shapes and sizes but essentially there are two main designs – *lean-to* with a flat or sloping roof, and *multi-sided* with a pitched roof.
Lean-to conservatories are generally

simple in design and construction, fairly small in area and at the less expensive end of the scale. Typically they are added to the outside wall of a living room or kitchen where there is an existing door, but equally they can go against a solid wall with access from the outside only. DIY construction is often a possibility.

Multi-sided conservatories tend to be larger; they are more like an extra room, entered through a door, french windows or their own passageway. They are generally much more expensive and usually require professional erection, though this is often included in the price.

Both types are available through the major DIY stores, as well as being made and installed by replacement window companies. Many manufacturers have show sites where you can inspect examples.

You could also consider custom-building (see panel opposite).

Providing a base

Whether you are assembling the conservatory yourself or getting it put up professionally, it will be your responsibility to provide a proper base. In most cases, the base will consist of a 100mm (4″) thick concrete slab topped by a damp-proof membrane and 50mm (2″) screed, though on clay or sandy soil you should lay this over 100mm (4″) of well compacted hardcore.

The conservatory manufacturers may offer a base-laying service, but this won't be included in any all-in price you get quoted. Alternatively, you might want to leave the job to a builder even if you are building the rest of the conservatory yourself.

Glass and safety

The large areas of glass in most conservatories can be a hazard, especially where there is direct entry from the house and there are small children running from room to room. So if you are planning to use the conservatory as living space – rather than just for growing plants – make sure it comes with proper safety glass, particularly at the lower levels.

There are two main types of safety glass. *Toughened glass* is up to five times stronger than normal glass, and if it does break it does so into tiny harmless fragments. *Laminated glass* consists of a thin layer of plastic sandwiched between layers of ordinary glass; it can be broken, but the plastic layer ensures the cracked panes remain intact.

LEAN-TO CONSERVATORIES

Most lean-to conservatories consist of fully glazed aluminium-framed panels, topped by a similarly glazed sloping roof which meets the walls at an angle or forms a continuous curve. They generally have sliding doors, though outward opening hinged ones are also available. There is a choice of single or double glazing.

Timber-framed lean-tos also use a panel construction, but tend to have the lower halves clad with weatherboarding leaving only the upper halves glazed. Alternatively, fully glazed half-height panels may sit on low brick walls or separate panels of reinforced concrete. Roofs are more likely to be translucent plastic sheeting than glass, and doors are usually hinged.

Lean-tos of all kinds are generally supplied as modular kits. Most come in standard sizes but some manufacturers will make up specific sized panels to order.

If self-assembly is an option, the main points to ensure are that the panels are fully weathertight, and that the junctions with the house wall don't bridge the damp-proof course or create penetrating damp problems later on. The alternative is to take advantage of the maker's erection service, which will add around 10% to the basic cost.

MULTI-SIDED CONSERVATORIES

Multi-sided conservatories fall into two categories. Traditional 'Victorian' designs are available mainly in timber and uPVC, and have a pitched roof which fans out to meet the angled front walls. Modern designs come in uPVC and aluminium, with flat roofs and a curved fascia that gives a more rounded effect at the front. Both can often be individually tailored to blend in with a particular style of house, but they are generally much more expensive than lean-tos.

Normally, but not always, multi-sided conservatories are built on a low brick wall, and features include shaped windows, gutter-level friezes and ridge finials. With the grandest designs there is no limit on size – you could even have an L shaped structure enclosing the entire back of the house, though at this level a conservatory begins to equate with a full-blown extension in terms of planning control, building time and expense.

Eight end panels form a curved end to this uPVC/aluminium frame.

False glazing bars give a Georgian look (above) whereas wood and brick (right) give a more authentic effect.

Lean-to conservatories are available in kit form (for assembly yourself or by the supplier), or made-to-measure. The materials for construction include glazed uPVC frames fitted to a low brick wall (left), aluminium frames (top), and hardwood frames (above).

CUSTOM BUILDING

There is no reason why you can't get a conservatory custom designed and built by an architect and a firm of local builders. The main advantages are that the shape and materials can be selected to blend perfectly with the house, and you will be less restricted in terms of size. The conservatory could also be tailored to fit an awkward space.

Against this, building from scratch means you are unlikely to be able to take advantage of modern maintenance-free materials such as aluminium or uPVC. And if the builder uses standard glazed panels, the chances are a replacement window manufacturer could do the same for less money.

ON THE ROOF?

If you have a suitable flat roof, perhaps already in use as a terrace, there is no reason why you shouldn't put the conservatory there. In fact, first floor 'winter gardens' were very popular in Victorian and Edwardian times.

You will need an architect or surveyor to confirm that the roof timbers are strong enough to take this extra load. But if the roof is already in use as a terrace, the chances are it can bear the weight of a small conservatory as well.

PRACTICAL POINTS

Once you have settled on what sort of conservatory you want, there will be practical decisions to make concerning services, decoration and furnishings.

Power and lighting

No conservatory should be without an electricity supply, and it's sensible to work out in advance where you want sockets and switches so that the wiring can be built into the structure. It should be simple enough to extend the downstairs power circuit to provide one or two sockets in the new building, but since these are likely to power garden equipment, it's worth protecting the circuit (or at least the sockets) with *residual current circuit breakers* (RCCBs).

The roof design of many conservatories makes it impossible or undesirable to have pendant lights. A popular alternative is to have wall mounted spots powered from socket outlets via curly flexes. Other possibilities include floor-standing uplighters, which look particularly good if arranged to shine through plant displays.

Heating

Although there will be enough natural heat in a conservatory for most of the year, you may need a top-up during the winter months. Winter heating also extends the range of plants you can cultivate.

One possibility is to add an extra radiator on to the existing central heating system – if the conservatory is double glazed, it won't matter if this goes on what was an outside

A serviceable tiled floor, easily adjustable blinds and wicker furniture are practical and attractive.

wall. Another economical option is an electric storage heater, preferably wired up to an Economy 7 meter to take advantage of the cheap night-time tariff.

Providing shade

While the main idea of a conservatory is to have a warm sun-filled room, there may be times when it gets too bright or too hot for comfort. Either install roller blinds or greenhouse shades at roof level inside the conservatory, or have a special conservatory awning fitted outside to cover the roof. Most conservatory manufacturers supply blinds as optional extras.

Good ventilation also helps keep down the temperature in high summer. Panels should include plenty of opening windows, vents and louvres. Some manufacturers offer automatic openers which operate when the temperature reaches a certain level.

Windows are essential for ventilation in sunny weather. Check they close securely if the conservatory is used for storage.

Flooring

Your choice of flooring depends mainly on use. The traditional options – paving slabs, or ceramic or quarry tiles – still hold good if you plan to use the conservatory mainly as a garden room or plant growing area. Woodstrip flooring is a warmer option, but may warp if it regularly gets wet. For a living or play area, vinyl tiles offer a good compromise between comfort and practicality.

Furniture and furnishing

Garden-type furniture in white timber or plastic, cane, or wrought iron suits a conservatory best, while furnishings and upholstery tend to look most effective with a bias towards the colour green.

For growing and displaying plants, choose from the wide range of products available from garden centres or from the conservatory manufacturers themselves. These vary from utilitarian aluminium 'greenhouse' staging to more elegant slatted timber shelving systems; keep them to the edges so that space is left inside for living.

INDEX

ACKNOWLEDGEMENTS

Photographers
Alton 25; Amoega 77(bl); Arcaid (Ian Bruce) front cover(tr), 1(tl); Baco 76(c); Banbury 70(t), 70(b), 71(t), 77(cl); BCA 20, 28, 45(t); Butterley 21; Cement & Concrete Association 33; Continental Awnings 38(b); Eric Crichton 31(b); Geoff Dann 30-31(t); Eaglemoss (Jon Bouchier) front cover(tl) 15, 30(l), (Derek St Romaine) 62-63, (Steve Tanner) 7, 50; ECC Quarries 41; Forest Fencing 53; The Garden Picture Library 29, 38(t), 39, 66, (Brian Carter) 4, (John McCarthy) 2, (Jerry Pavia) front cover(br); HSS Hire Shops 44; IMI Opella 11; Larch Lap 54-55(t), 65, 70(c);

Marshalls 45(br), 48; Monarch Aluminium 30(b); Regal Sheds 71(c); Sun 76(b); Wessex 75, 77(t), 78(b); Elizabeth Whiting Associates 37, 54(c), 59, 72, 77(cr), 77(br), (Michael Dunne) 6, (Jerry Harpur) 1(r); Wickes 45(bl), 55(c), 69, 71(b), 76(t), 78(t).

Illustrators
Paul Emra 15-18, 25-28, 33-36, 45-48, 49-52; Jeremy Gower 53-58; Andrew Green 7-10, 11-14, 29-32, 53-58; Maltings Partnership front cover(bl), 19-20, 37-40, 41-44, 69-74; Mark Franklin 25-28; Stan North; 21-24, 59-64, 65-68; Peter Serjeant 29-32, 33-36, 41-44, 53-58; Steve Tonkin 15-18, 33-36; Paul Williams 7-10.